# MEL BAY'S COMPLETE BLUES BASS BOOK

## By Mike Hiland

---

### ONLINE AUDIO

| | | | |
|---|---|---|---|
| 1 Tuning-Open G | 9 Ex. 3.8 | Ex. 4.29 | Ex. 5.36 [1:09] |
| Tuning-Open D | Ex. 3.9 | Ex. 4.30 [1:47] | 26 Ex. 5.37 |
| Tuning-Open A | Ex. 3.11 | 18 Ex. 4.31 | Ex. 5.39 |
| Tuning-Open E [:42] | Ex. 3.12 | Ex. 4.35 | Ex. 5.40 [1:05] |
| 2 Ex. 1.2-Key of C | Ex. 3.15 [2:14] | Ex. 4.36 | 27 Ex. 5.42 |
| Ex. 1.2-Key of F | 10 Ex. 4.2 | Ex. 5.37 [2:19] | Ex. 5.45 [:48] |
| Ex. 1.2-Key of B♭ | Ex. 4.3 | 19 Ex. 5.3 | 28 Ex. 6.1 [1:19] |
| Ex. 1.2-Key of A | Ex. 4.4 [2:19] | Ex. 5.4 | 29 Ex. 6.4 [1:21] |
| Ex. 1.4-Key of C | 11 Ex. 4.6 | Ex. 5.6 [:53] | 30 Ex. 6.5 [1:13] |
| Ex. 1.4-Key of F | Ex. 4.7 | 20 Ex. 5.7 | 31 Ex. 6.6 [2:12] |
| Ex. 1.4-Key of B♭ | Ex. 4.8 [2:02] | Ex. 5.8 | 32 Ex. 6.7 [1:07] |
| Ex. 1.4-Key of A [1:36] | 12 Ex. 4.9 | Ex. 5.9 [1:00] | 33 Ex. 6.9 [1:11] |
| 3 Ex. 1.5 | Ex. 4.12 [1:05] | 21 Ex. 5.10 | 34 Ex. 6.11 [1:12] |
| Ex. 1.9 [1:20] | 13 Ex. 4.13 | Ex. 5.11 | 35 Ex. 6.12 [1:15] |
| 4 Ex. 1.14 | Ex. 4.14 | 22 Ex. 5.13 | 36 Ex. 6.13 [1:02] |
| Ex. 1.17 [:33] | Ex. 4.16 [1:43] | Ex. 5.14 | 37 Ex. 6.14 [1:09] |
| 5 Ex. 1.18 | 14 Ex. 4.17 | Ex. 5.15 [:50] | 38 Ex. 6.15 [1:54] |
| Ex. 1.20 [1:17] | Ex. 4.18 [1:34] | 23 Ex. 5.16 | 39 Ex. 6.19 [1:18] |
| 6 Ex. 1.22 | 15 Ex. 4.20 | Ex. 5.17 | 40 Ex. 6.20 [1:27] |
| Ex. 1.23 [:33] | Ex. 4.21 | Ex. 5.19 [:46] | 41 Ex. 6.21 [2:17] |
| 7 Ex. 2.1 | Ex. 4.23 [2:47] | 24 Ex. 5.28 | 42 Ex. 6.24 [1:39] |
| Ex. 2.5 [1:34] | 16 Ex. 4.24 | Ex. 5.29 | 43 Ex. 6.36 [2:19] |
| 8 Ex. 3.1 | Ex. 4.25 | Ex. 5.30 [:51] | 44 Ex. 6.37 [1:39] |
| Ex. 3.3 | Ex. 4.26 [2:12] | 25 Ex. 5.34 | 45 Ex. 6.38 [2:50] |
| Ex. 3.4 | 17 Ex. 4.27 | Ex. 5.35 | 46 Ex. 6.40 [2:00] |
| Ex. 3.6 [2:07] | | | |

## To Access the Online Audio Go To:
### *www.melbay.com/95403MEB*

# Table of Contents

**DEFINITIONS** ...................................................................................................**4**

    Fretboard Diagram ..................................................................... 4

    Music and Tablature .................................................................. 4

**BASIC BLUES CONCEPTS** ................................................................ **6**

    Major Scale Walking Pattern ..................................................... 6

    Mixolydian Walking Pattern ....................................................... 8

    The Basic 12-Bar Blues Progression ...................................... 10

    Playing The Blues .................................................................... 12

    Basic Blues Grooves ............................................................... 20

    More Blues ............................................................................... 23

    Playing Techniques .................................................................. 27

**SCALES AND CHORDS** ................................................................. **30**

    Major Scales ............................................................................ 30

    The Mixolydian Scale ............................................................... 35

    Minor Pentatonic Scales .......................................................... 40

    The Minor Blues Scale ............................................................. 45

    The Altered Blues Scale ........................................................... 50

    Chord Types ............................................................................. 55

**BLUES PROGRESSIONS** ............................................................... **58**

    Basic 12-Bar Progressions ...................................................... 58

    12-Bar Variations .................................................................... 59

    8-Bar Blues ............................................................................. 66

    16-Bar Blues ........................................................................... 69

    Minor Blues Progressions ........................................................ 71

**BLUES STYLES** ........................................................................... **75**

    Texas Swing ............................................................................. 77

    Texas Shuffle ........................................................................... 82

    Jump Blues .............................................................................. 85

    Chicago Blues .......................................................................... 89

    Rhythm And Blues .................................................................... 94

    Slow Blues Styles .................................................................... 98

    Rock Blues ............................................................................. 102

    Jazz Blues ............................................................................. 110

**INTROS, ENDINGS, TURNAROUNDS, AND FILLS** ...................... **120**

    Intros ..................................................................................... 120

    Fills ........................................................................................ 126

    Turnarounds ........................................................................... 132

    Endings .................................................................................. 134

**ADVANCED BLUES BASS LINES** ............................................... **138**

    Blues Review .......................................................................... 138

    Puttin' It All Together .............................................................. 174

**NOW WHAT?** ............................................................................ **194**

**APPENDIX A** ............................................................................. **195**

# Foreword

So, you wanna play the blues? Well, good! You'll find that the blues can be one of the most emotionally rewarding styles of music to play. As I write this book, I have been playing the bass guitar for over 20 years and I can honestly tell you that without a doubt the most satisfying gigs for me have always been blues gigs. There is nothing like coming home in the early morning hours feeling absolutely emotionally drained after playing music all night. That's when you know you gave it your all. And if you do this, the blues will give something back to you.

After going through this entire book, you will have a thorough understanding of the chord structure and theory behind blues bass lines. The element that I can't show you in a book is the feeling you strive to create when you play the blues. However, when you understand the structure of blues songs and bass lines well enough that you don't even have to think about what to play or what the next chord is, then your mind is free to concentrate on creating the right feel or mood for the song. Then you too can come home at three o'clock in the morning with that *"been playing the blues all night"* smile on your face!

The blues is typically thought of as sad songs about love gone bad. The truth is that blues songs talk about things that we can all relate to: happiness, sorrow and everything in between. The good blues musician can convey the message in the lyrics into a feeling through his or her instrument. That's why we play the blues; to share those feelings with the audience. And, everyone gets to contribute: the singer, the guitar player, the drummer, and yes, even the bass player. I had the pleasure of seeing Buddy Guy play live the other night. I have never seen a room full of happier people! Just a bunch of sad songs? I don't think so!

It is not my intention to provide you with a history of the blues. Through the course of this book, I will explain where some of the different styles originated and who some of the artists associated with specific styles of the blues are, but that is not the main focus of this book. The objective is to teach you the fundamental concepts of blues bass playing. We will also talk about how to expand on those ideas in an effort to create different feels and grooves.

If you've been playing bass for a while, there's a good chance that you have already played blues songs at one time or another. This was the case with me. If someone called a blues song or progression, I could get through it without too much trouble. It wasn't until a number of years ago that I became very interested in really learning and understanding what the blues was all about. I owe this to the late Stevie Ray Vaughan. He was able to get my attention and get me curious. In reading about him, I saw names like Buddy Guy, Albert King, Freddie King, T-Bone Walker and many others. The more I liked Stevie, the more I went out and bought records by the artists who had influenced him. That's all it took: I was hooked.

Before we get going, I want to dedicate this book to Stevie Ray Vaughan. His life may have been cut short, but he left me with a lifetime of inspiration and an understanding of what a gift it is to be a musician that I am forever in his debt. With any luck, some of that may now be passed on to you. Good Luck ... Mike H.

# Definitions

**FRETBOARD DIAGRAM** .........................................................................................

Before we actually start learning and playing, let's take a look at some of the graphics objects you will see in this book. When we talk about scales and where they are found on the fretboard, I am using a "Fretboard Diagram" to help illustrate where to play the notes on the fingerboard. Typically, I will only show the starting position for a particular scale. From there, you can use the written music and tablature (see page 5), as well as your own understanding of the fretboard and music theory to find the scale in other locations up and down the neck.

The Fretboard Diagram is explained below. It shows a section of the fretboard (usually a 5-fret area) and uses horizontal lines to indicate the strings and vertical lines to indicate the frets. String names and fret numbers are provided for reference. The notes in the scale are indicated by "scale tone numbers", with the root of the scale surrounded by a square while other scale tones are contained in circles. Always refer to the written music when looking at a Fretboard Diagram to insure that you understand the note names as well as the scale tone numbers. Remember, it is important to learn the notes in the scale, not just memorize the pattern in the diagram.

## Fretboard Diagram

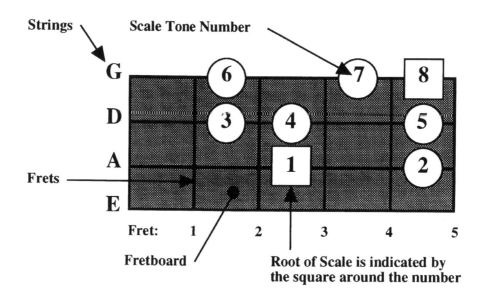

**MUSIC AND TABLATURE** ...................................................................................

The other type of diagram used in this book is in the form of written music and tablature. Because we are dealing with chord progressions as well as bass lines, it may be necessary to explain some of the information contained in the musical examples.

In addition to the bass lines, which are written in standard notation, I have included tablature to indicate the strings and fret numbers that I had in mind when I wrote the example. IT IS NOT NECESSARY THAT YOU PLAY THESE EXAMPLES IN THE SAME LOCATION AS THE TABLATURE. Tablature is used as an aid when reading music. Once you learn and understand each example, try it in different areas of the fretboard. Not only will this help you learn your fingerboard, but you may find that you like the sound of certain notes in other parts of the neck.

In addition to the bass lines and tablature, there are chord names indicated above the staff and in some cases, chord numbers are also included. If you don't understand what the chord numbers are, read the following "Basic Blues Concepts" chapter and that should clear it up for you.

I have also included chord tone numbers in many examples to indicate how each note in the bass line is related to the chord being played at that time. This is a very important concept and you should strive to have a complete understanding of how each note you play relates to the current chord. This will allow you to create your own bass lines later on.

# Music and Tablature Diagram

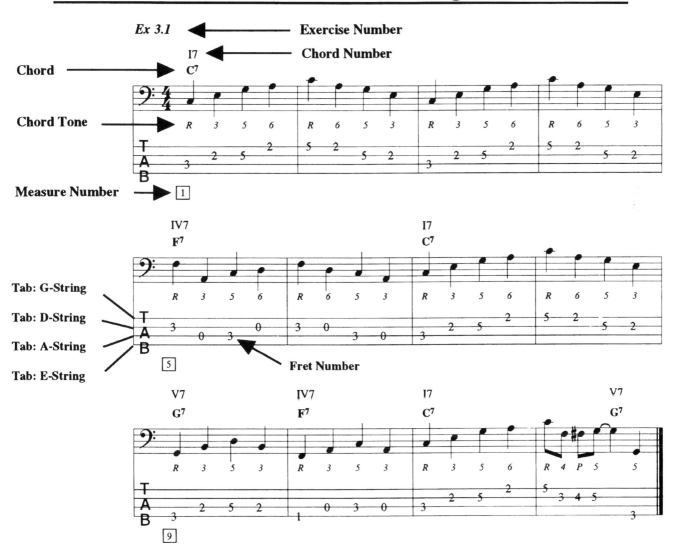

# Basic Blues Concepts

In this chapter, we are going to discuss the two basic types of blues walking bass lines you will encounter. We will also take a look at the basic chord progression that is used in the blues. Future chapters will expand on these concepts, but we want to get you playing right away!

Blues bass lines typically fall under two categories: major and mixolydian. This means that the notes you are playing are either taken from the major scale or from the mixolydian scale.

**MAJOR SCALE WALKING PATTERN** ...................................................................................

The first type of walking bass line we are going to look at is based on the major scale, and uses four notes from that scale: Root, 3rd, 5th, and 6th. This type of walking pattern typically starts at a lower octave of the root and then "walks" up the 3rd, 5th, and 6th scale tones. Then you go back down those notes this time starting at the upper octave of the root, then the 6th, 5th, and 3rd. Figure 1.1 shows you the fretboard diagram for the C Major Scale. Exercise 1.1 shows you the written notation for the C Major Scale. The scale tones we will be concerned with are circled (between the staff and tablature).

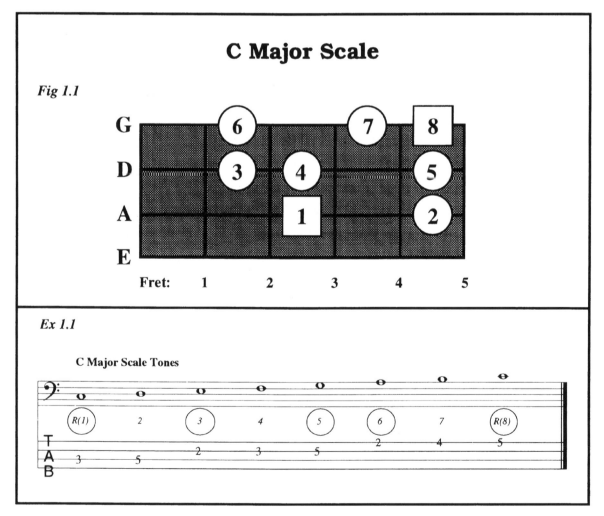

Here are some examples of this type of major scale walking bass line in four different keys (meaning they are based on four different scales): C, F, B♭, and A major. Practice each of these bass lines in each of the four keys shown.

I want you to notice that they are the exact same "fingering pattern" in each key. This means that they are *movable* patterns! They can be played anywhere on the neck <u>in any key</u> by simply moving the root note (which is indicated by the capital 'R' in the scale tone area below each note). If you start with D as the root (A-string, 5th fret) and play that same fingering pattern, you will be playing the bass line in the key of D major. Get it?

This concept is very important as blues songs are written and played in all keys. You must be able to apply the different types of walking bass lines we will discuss in this book to any key at any time! That's a tall order, so be sure you really understand each pattern before proceeding to the next section.

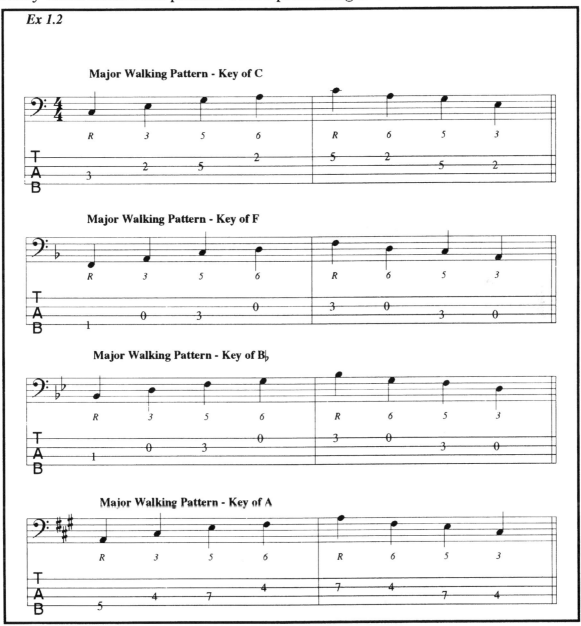

*Ex 1.2*

Major Walking Pattern - Key of C

Major Walking Pattern - Key of F

Major Walking Pattern - Key of B♭

Major Walking Pattern - Key of A

The other common walking bass line is derived from the Mixolydian mode. This needs some explanation. The scale you will see below is formally known as the C Mixolydian mode. Without going into the theory too deeply, this means that it contains the notes from the F Major Scale, starting and ending on the fifth note of the F scale, which is C. That's what mixolydian means in a nutshell.

Due to its widespread use, it has earned a few other names. The mixolydian mode is also known as: the mixolydian scale, the dominant scale, and the seventh-chord scale. Here's how we need to think about it as blues bass players: It is the C Major Scale with a lowered (or flat) 7th scale tone. A picture is worth a thousand words at this point so take a look at Figure 1.2 below and play the scale as shown. Notice that the only difference between this scale pattern and the major scale pattern is that the 7th tone has been lowered by one half-step to B♭. That is the only difference. For our purposes in this book, we will refer to this as the Mixolydian Scale.

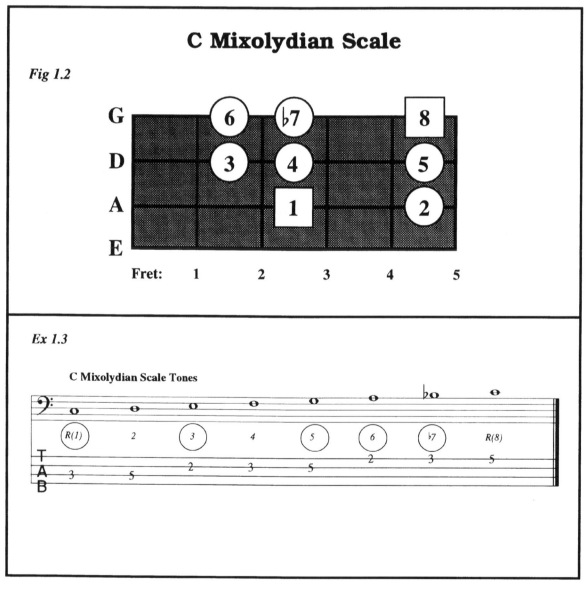

# C Mixolydian Scale

*Fig 1.2*

*Ex 1.3*

C Mixolydian Scale Tones

Here are some examples of the mixolydian walking pattern in four keys: C, F, B♭, and A. The noticeable difference between this pattern and the major walking pattern is that this pattern starts at the lower octave of the root, then goes to the 3rd, 5th, and 6th just like the major walking pattern. The difference comes in that you don't go all the way to the upper octave of the root. Instead, you go to the ♭7 and then proceed back down to the 6th, 5th, and 3rd.

Again, notice that this is also a movable pattern that can be played in any key, anywhere on the neck. Be sure to practice this pattern thoroughly as it is a very important part of playing blues bass.

## THE BASIC 12-BAR BLUES PROGRESSION

All blues songs are based on a simple progression using three chords. There can be many variations on this progression, but it is absolutely imperative that you understand the basic 12-bar blues progression in order to be prepared for and understand the variations.

The chords used in blues progressions are usually referred to by number. These numbers will be indicated in Roman Numeral form (usually). In this book, I will indicate the chord number by placing the Roman Numeral equivalent above the name of the chord in the music staff. (See the definition on page 5 for clarification if needed.)

Again, I don't want to stray into a theory discussion about why certain chords are major and others are minor, but we must have a basic understanding so that we know what to expect of the chords in a given progression.

The chords are usually based on the notes in the major scale. We will use the C major scale as an example since it is the easiest to deal with (no sharps or flats). The chords that are created by the notes in the major scale have the same chord number (Roman Numeral) as the number of the scale tone that is the root of each chord. This means that the C chord is called "I", the D chord is called "II", the E chord is "III", etc....

Due to the intervals between notes in those chords, some of the chords are major and others are minor. In major chords, the 3rd is located two whole-steps above the root. In minor chords, the 3rd is lowered by one half-step and is therefore found one-and-a-half steps above the root. The 5th is always a perfect 5th, except for the VII chord which has a flat 5 (lowered by one half-step).

All of these chords consist of four basic notes from the scale. They are the root, 3rd, 5th and 7th. In some cases that means major or minor 3rd. In all cases the 7th is a flat 7 (lowered by one half-step). *(NOTE: Technically, the four chord (IV) should be a "major seventh" chord since the 7th is located one half-step below the root. But the blues don't dig that "major seven" sound, so the IV chord almost always uses a flat seven.)* Major chords with a flat 7th are called "dominant 7" or "dominant" chords (i.e. C dominant 7, C dominant) and are written as "C7". Minor chords with a flat 7th are called "minor seven" chords (i.e. D minor seven, E minor seven) and are written as Dm7 or Em7. The minor chord with a flat 7 and a flat 5 is called a "minor seven flat five" or "half-diminished" chord and is written as Bm7♭5.

Figure 1.3 shows you the order of dominant and minor seven chords in the key of C major. (**NOTE**: The major chords are indicated by an upper case Roman Numeral (I7, IV7, V7) and minor chords are indicated by lower case Roman Numerals (iim7 is read "two-minor-seven") THIS ORDER OF CHORDS IS TRUE FOR ANY AND ALL MAJOR KEYS. This is why numbers are used to indicate chords. Once you are familiar with the chord numbering system, you can quickly understand a chord progression in any key. You just need to associate the chord number with the notes in the major scale and you will then know the chords used in any progression.

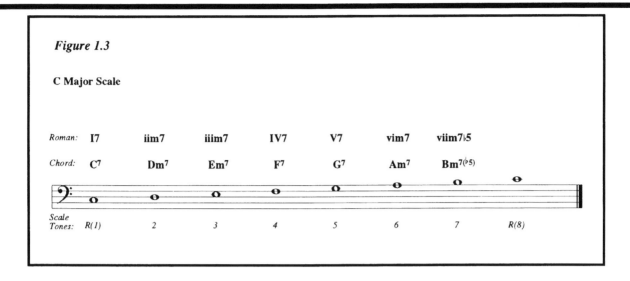

Figure 1.3

C Major Scale

| Roman: | I7 | iim7 | iiim7 | IV7 | V7 | vim7 | viim7♭5 |
|--------|-----|-------|--------|------|------|--------|----------|
| Chord: | C7 | Dm7 | Em7 | F7 | G7 | Am7 | Bm7(♭5) |
| Scale Tones: | R(1) | 2 | 3 | 4 | 5 | 6 | 7 | R(8) |

The basic 12-bar blues chord progression uses the I7, IV7, and V7 chords from the scale that the song is based on. Let's keep talking about the key of C for simplicity. The I7, IV7, and V7 chords in the key of C (according to Fig 1.3) are as follows: C7, F7, and G7. Those three chords are then arranged into an order that makes up the 12 measures (or bars) that is the basic 12-bar blues progression.

Figure 1.4 shows you the order of the I7, IV7, and V7 chords in the basic 12-bar blues progression. By learning the Roman Numerals in this figure, you can then plug in the appropriate chords from any key and have the blues progression for that key. Now we're gettin' somewhere - you have just learned 12 blues songs!

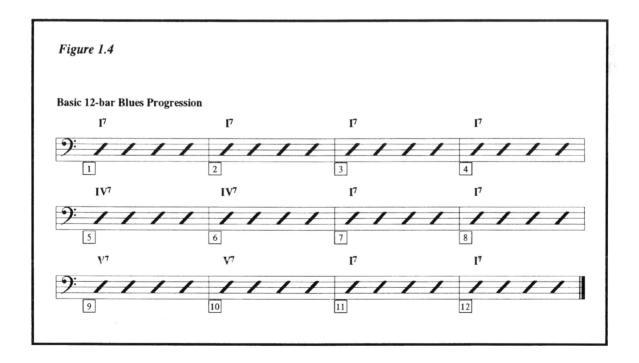

Figure 1.4

Basic 12-bar Blues Progression

## PLAYING THE BLUES ...................................................................................................

Exercises 1.5, 1.6, 1.7, and 1.8 are examples of the major walking pattern as used in the basic 12-bar blues progression in four different keys. Pay particular attention to the chord tone numbers shown below each note. These numbers indicate the notes relationship to the current <u>chord</u> (R = Root, 3 = 3rd, 5 = 5th, 6 = 6th), not the scale.

One way to think of this is that the current chord is based on the root of the scale with the same name. I'll explain.... Against the C7 chord, you are playing the Root, 3rd, 5th and 6th chord tones. If you play the C Mixolydian pattern we learned earlier you will see that these notes are also the Root, 3rd, 5th, and 6th tones of that scale pattern. Get it? When you are playing against a dominant 7 chord (i.e. C7), you can visualize the mixolydian scale pattern for the chord to help identify the notes that are available to you. This will become clearer as we go.

For now, let's start playing the blues....

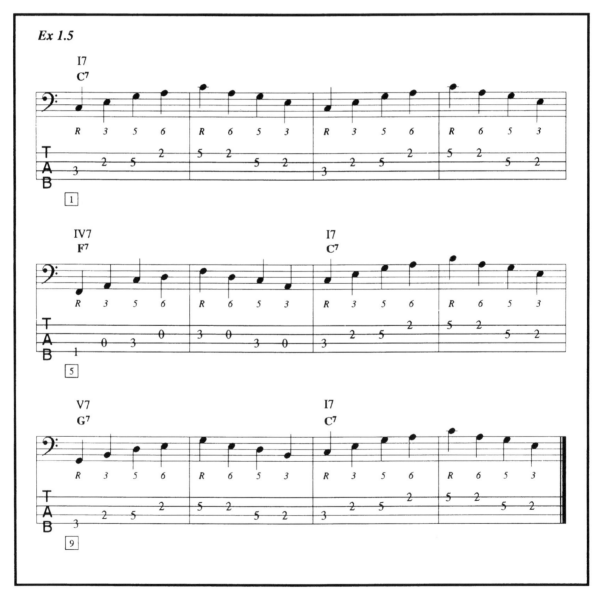

## Ex 1.6

*Ex 1.7*

*Ex 1.8*

Exercises 1.9, 1.10, 1.11, and 1.12 are examples of the mixolydian walking pattern as used in the basic 12-bar blues progression in the same four keys as before.

Again, pay attention to the chord tone numbers indicated below each note. Try playing this progression in some other keys when you get comfortable with these four exercises.

**Ex 1.10**

*Ex 1.11*

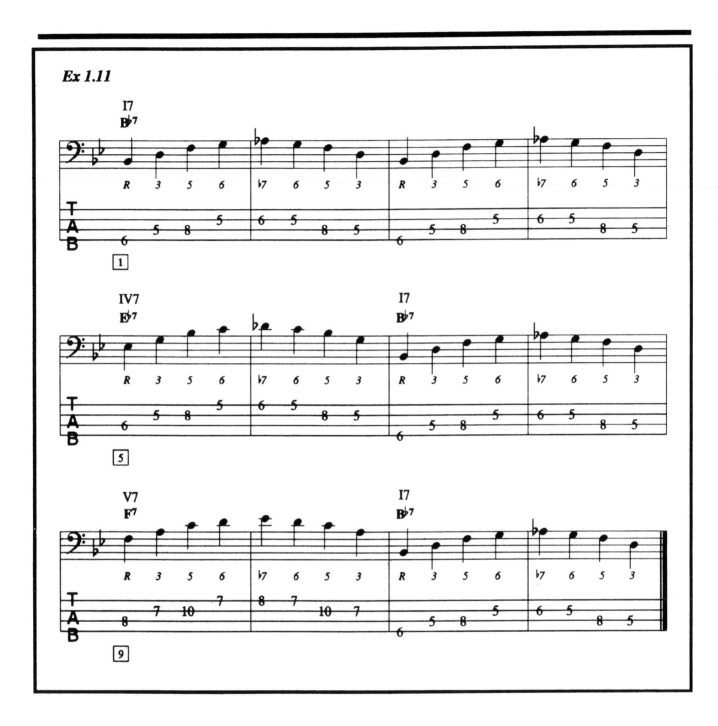

*Ex 1.12*

**BASIC BLUES GROOVES** ............................................................................

So far, all of our examples have been bass lines using quarter notes. There are a few different types of rhythm figures that you will encounter and use as you play the blues. In this section, we take a look at the four most common rhythms and one that is not so common, but you should know about it anyway.

First, we'll look at the quarter note rhythm using the major walking pattern as an example. Each note is played right on each beat. The time signature is almost always 4/4 when you are playing a quarter note pattern. Exercise 1.13 shows how it is written.

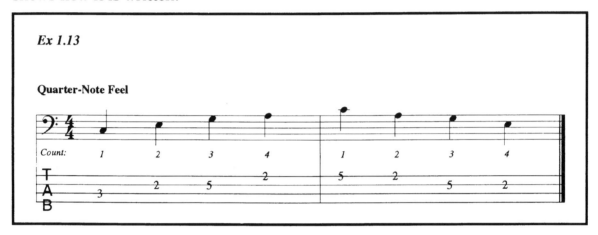

Exercise 1.14 shows the same walking pattern played as eighth notes. This is a straight eighth note feel, not a swing or a shuffle. We'll talk about those in a minute.

Eighth notes ring for one-half of a beat and are counted as "one-and-two-and-three-and-four-and" as shown in Exercise 1.14 below. Make sure that you are playing all of the notes evenly as you practice this exercise. Each note should be as loud as the next. You must be able to play evenly if necessary. You can learn to emphasize certain notes later after you are more comfortable with the note selection. For now, concentrate on a smooth even attack on each note.

Exercise 1.15 is the one rhythm figure that is rarely used, but it should be documented so that you are aware of its existence and understand the difference between it and the more common shuffle rhythms. This exercise uses a dotted eighth note/sixteenth note combination to create a shuffle feel.

A simple description of a "shuffle" feel is that there is a pickup note before each beat. Now, this example certainly fits that description. However, it is a little stiff in comparison to the rhythm figures that are based on a triplet feel which we will begin discussing next. First, let's take a look at Exercise 1.15.

One of the more common shuffle rhythms is written in 12/8 time. This means that there are twelve beats per measure (yes, you have to count to 12!) and that the eighth note receives one full beat instead of its usual one-half beat value. The end result is that you have a rhythm that *feels* like four groups of three notes. This feels virtually the same as a triplet feel.

In fact, rather than count to twelve in each measure, you may find it easier to count in groups of three (one-two-three, two-two-three, three-two-three, four-two three). How you count is your own personal choice as long as you understand what you are counting. Exercise 1.16 is an example of a 12/8 shuffle feel. Notice that you play on the first note of each group of three notes (the 1st, 4th, 7th, and 10th beats) and there is a pickup note just before each of those beats. This is what creates the shuffle feel.

## Ex 1.16

For those of us who have a hard time counting to twelve over and over again without getting light-headed, this same type of shuffle feel can also be written in a 4/4 time signature. When the music is written in 4/4, the rhythm figures are actually four groups of eighth-note triplets. These would be counted as follows: one-trip-let, two-trip-let, three-trip-let, four-trip-let.

Now, if the music was actually written as four groups of eighth-note triplets, the written music may be as difficult to read as trying to count to twelve over and over in 12/8!! So, to make it easier to read the music, the notes are written as eighth notes and the following graphic is placed at the beginning of the piece of music to indicate that the triplet feel is to be used:

This graphic indicates that when you have two eighth notes written, they are to be played as follows: the length of the first eighth-note is as if the first two eighth-notes in the triplet were tied together; the second eighth-note is played where the third of those eighth-note triplets would be played. Exercise 1.17 should help you see this a little easier. This rhythm figure is probably the most common rhythm you will encounter when playing the blues, so make sure you understand it very well.

*Ex 1.17*

**Triplet Shuffle Feel**

## MORE BLUES

Exercises 1.18, 1.19, 1.20, and 1.21 are blues bass lines using our four "new" rhythm figures. Be sure to notice the triplet shuffle indicator at the beginning of Exercise 1.20! Try each exercise at a few different tempos to get used to the feel of each rhythm figure at different speeds. Also, keep paying attention to the volume of each note - make sure they are nice and even!

**Ex 1.18**

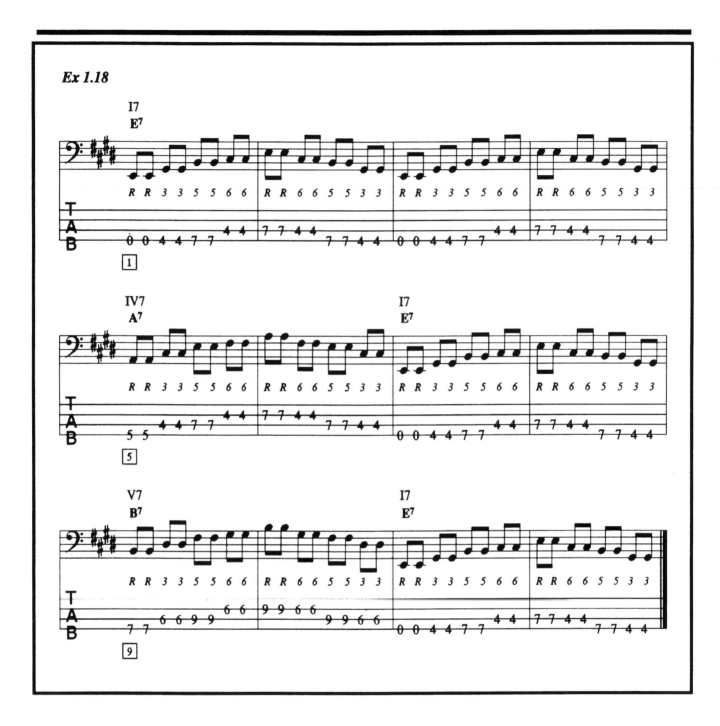

*Ex 1.19*

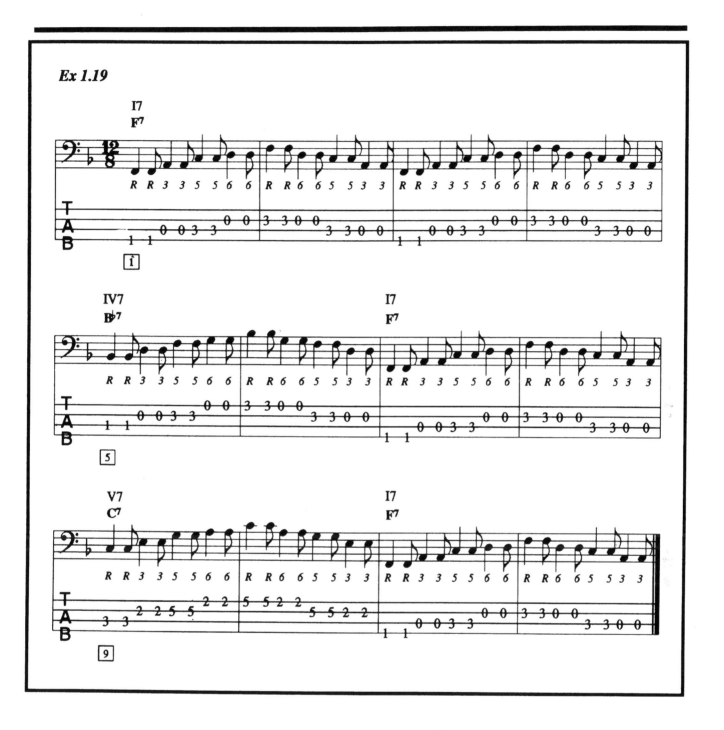

**Ex 1.20**

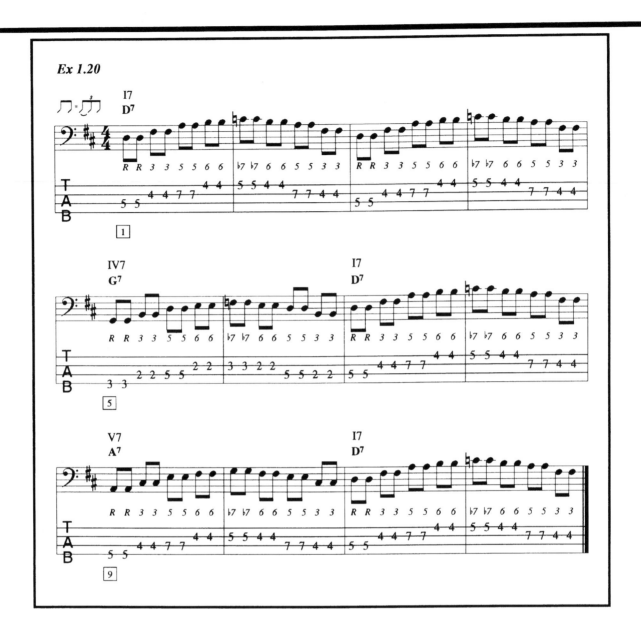

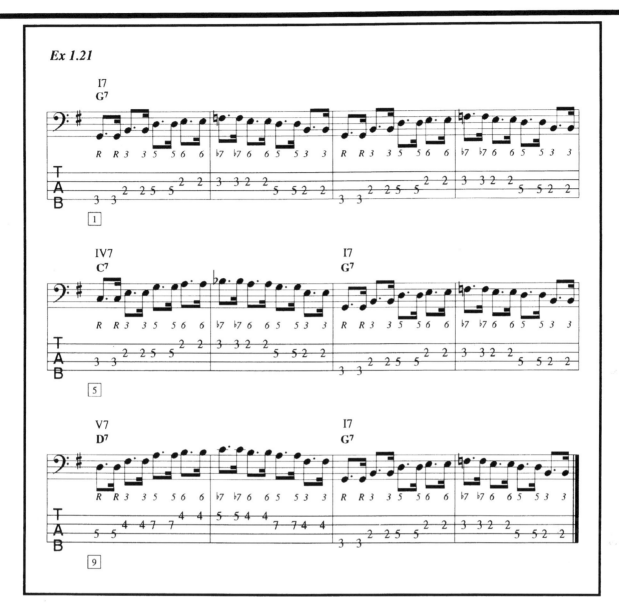

*Ex 1.21*

## PLAYING TECHNIQUES ................................................................................................

The final subject in this chapter deals with some of the playing techniques that you can use when playing the blues. First of all it should be pointed out that you can create different feels by varying how long each note rings before the next note is played. I'm not talking about quarter notes versus eighth notes versus sixteenth notes. I'm referring to whether or not you are playing with notes as "legato" or "staccato". Legato means that the notes ring nice and long for the full duration of their indicated note value. Staccato means that each note is cut short. The next note would be played at the correct time as indicated by the notation, but the notes don't necessarily ring for their full value. This creates more of a "jumpy" or "bouncy" kind of feel. Try experimenting with different approaches to notes and phrasing this way. Also, as you listen to records analyze how the bass player is playing those notes, not just which notes are being played. Remember, the blues is all about creating a feel or mood with the music. How you attack and sustain each note contributes to the overall feel of the song.

Beyond that, there are a couple of other techniques that are very common to blues bass playing. They are through the use of "dead notes" and in some cases open strings that are briefly played to create that shuffle feel. Exercises 1.22, 1.23, and 1.24 show you three different techniques you can use to help create movement in the rhythms you are playing. You will see examples of this as you go through this book.

Exercise 1.22 uses open-string pull-offs to create the shuffle feel. Be careful with this one. It is very easy to get out of control with the open strings and lose sight of the important notes (the chord tones played on the beat). Open-string pull-offs are executed by the left hand. Play the fretted note, then pull off of that note to the open string. Be careful not to let the open string ring too loudly or too long. Also, you must choose your open-string pull-offs wisely. If you are playing in flat keys (i.e. B♭, E♭, D♭, etc...) the open strings may not work too well harmonically. That means they may be wrong notes and sound very bad. That would not be good.

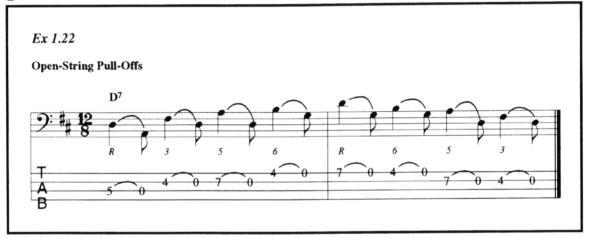

Exercise 1.23 uses dead notes that are picked with the right hand to help create the shuffle feel. Using dead notes is a technique that is common to many styles of music. When dead notes are written on the staff, they are written on the line or space corresponding to the open string that they are played on. I don't really care where your left hand is on the neck at the time of the dead note, but for picking ease, pay attention to which string you should be picking as the dead note.

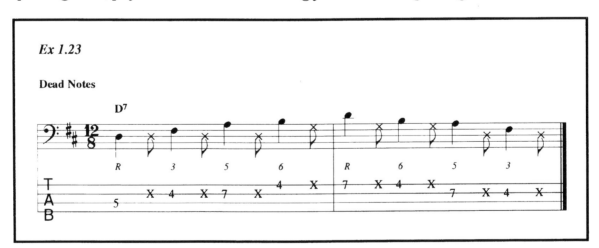

Exercise 1.24 is sort of a combination of Ex 1.22 and 1.23. You are pulling-off to dead notes, which will most likely be the open string. In order to achieve the dead note sound, you will probably have to mute the string with your right hand as well as your left when you execute the pull-off. Practice this exercise slowly to get the coordination right - it may take a few tries to get comfortable with it.

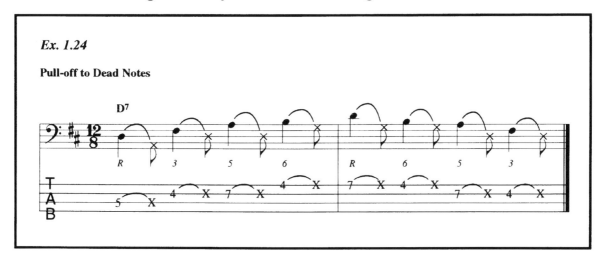

*Ex. 1.24*

**Pull-off to Dead Notes**

That does it for this chapter! Before we move on and talk a little scale and chord theory in the next chapter, you should make sure that you are comfortable with both of the walking bass patterns we have discussed: the major walking pattern and the mixolydian walking pattern. If you are still a little unsure, go back and practice those exercises some more.

Of even more importance is your understanding of the basic 12-bar blues progression. If you are not absolutely 100% comfortable with that concept, then go back and review it some more. It is the foundation that we will be building on throughout the remaining chapters. Make sure you can play the basic 12-bar progression in at least the four keys presented in this chapter, if not many more beyond that. *IT'S VERY IMPORTANT!!!*

# Scales and Chords

**MAJOR SCALES** ....................................................................................................

The first scale we should look at is the **major scale**. The major scale is the starting point or foundation for all of the other scales we will be discussing. In case you have never learned about scales, here is a brief explanation.

A major scale is defined as a series of eight notes, starting at the "root" note and ending at the same note played one octave higher. So, there are actually seven different notes in the scale, with the first and eighth notes being the same. All seven notes in the musical alphabet must be used once and only once. Therefore, the C major scale consists of the notes C, D, E, F, G, A, B, and C.

The intervals between those notes is what defines the scale as a *major* scale. The order of intervals is W-W-H-W-W-W-H, where "W" is a whole-step and "H" indicates a half-step. (Whole steps are two frets apart on the bass; Half steps are one fret apart)

Because we are expected to be able to play in any key (playing within a "key" means we are playing within the scale - i.e. the key of C is based on the C major scale), we must be able to quickly identify the notes in all twelve major scales. Once we can do that, the foundation of the song is laid out in front of us on the fingerboard and we can begin picking notes from the scale.

Figure 2.1 shows you the notes in the C major scale.

## C Major Scale

*Fig 2.1*

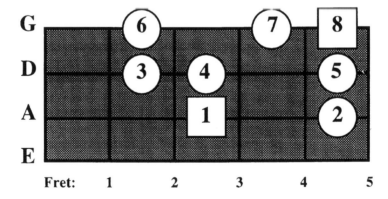

Figure 2.2 shows all twelve major scales in their standard location on the fingerboard. Basically that means that they are all played with the same fingering pattern. Once again, notice that this fingering pattern is essentially movable to any area of the fingerboard.

30

## Figure 2.2

### C Major Scale

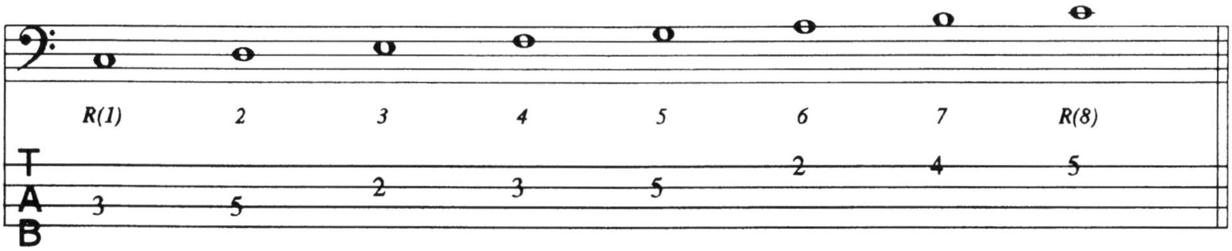

### F Major Scale

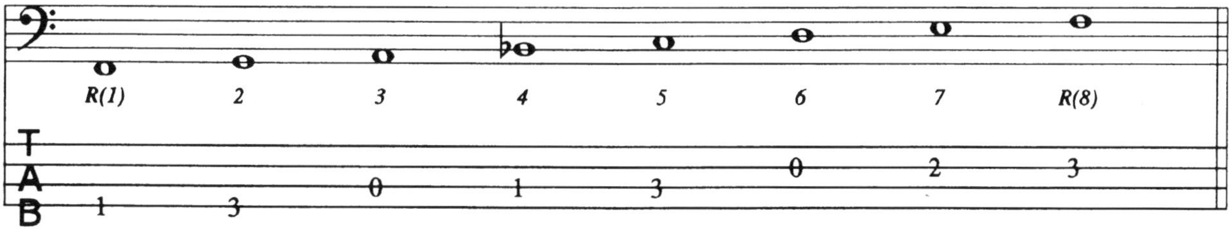

### B♭ Major Scale

### E♭ Major Scale

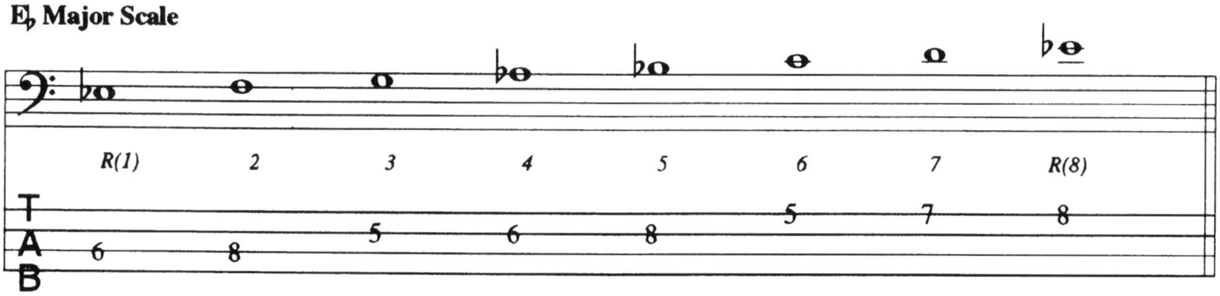

31

*Figure 2.2 (cont'd)*

**A♭ Major Scale**

**D♭ Major Scale**

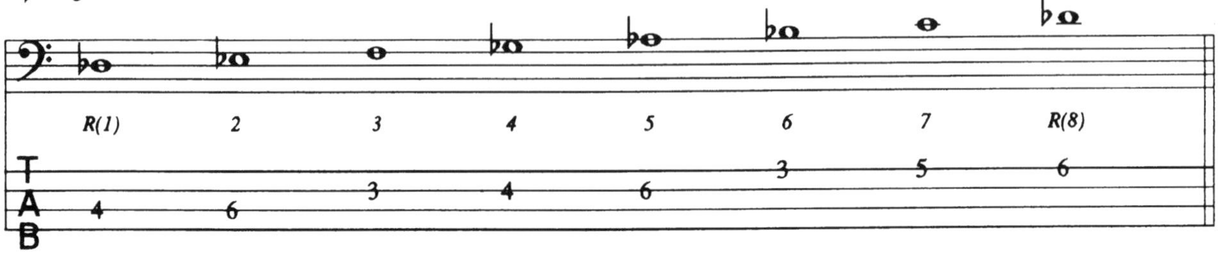

**F♯ Major Scale**

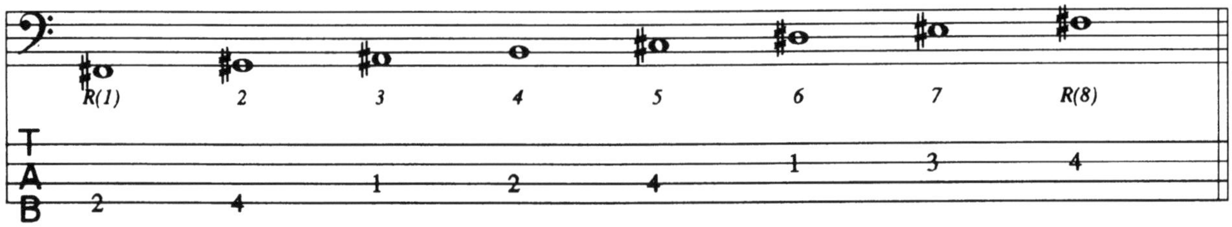

**B Major Scale**

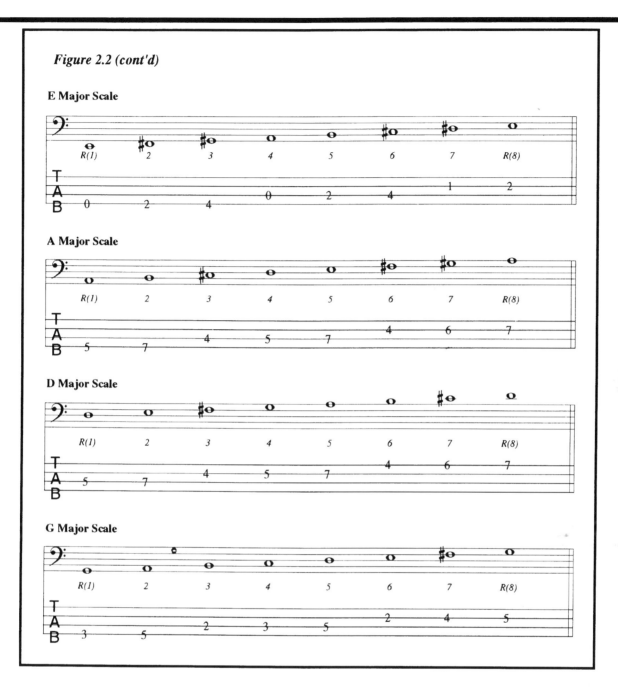

Figure 2.2 (cont'd)

E Major Scale

A Major Scale

D Major Scale

G Major Scale

Exercise 2.1 is a scale exercise to learn all of the notes in the C major scale in all positions on the fingerboard. Remember, the C major scale consists of seven notes: C, D, E, F, G, A, and B. Those notes are in the scale no matter where you are on the neck. In order to learn where those notes are, practice Exercise 2.1. This will show you how to find the notes in the C major scale from the nut all the way to the 12th fret.

After you learn the C major scale, try to apply the same concept to the other eleven scales. This is a monster exercise that will help you learn all of the notes in all of the scales in all positions on the fingerboard. Knock yourself out!

**Ex 2.1**

**C Major Scale Studies**

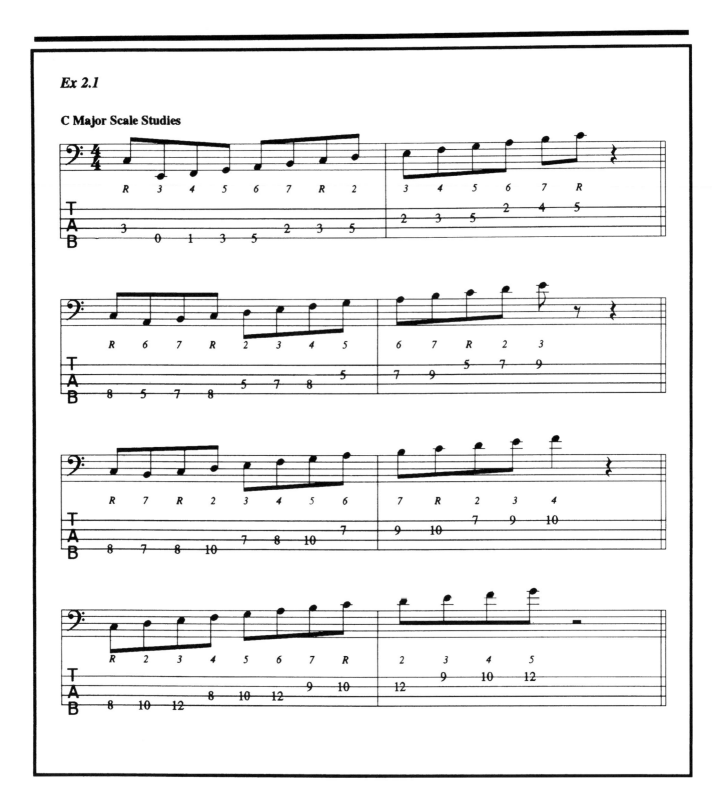

As I mentioned in the first chapter, the mixolydian mode is the source of many of the blues bass lines you will play. Rather than trying to figure out what key each mixolydian mode *really* belongs to, it is easier to think of these modes as the major scale with a lowered (flat) 7th. Therefore, we will be calling this scale **the mixolydian scale** for the remainder of this book.

The truth is you can think of any scale as being a modified major scale. (That's all they really are anyway!) Everything is based on the major scales, with some intervals being changed. In fact, these mixolydian scales can be thought of as the following series of intervals: W-W-H-W-W-H-W. So, don't think of the mixolydian as some new breed of scale; it's just a modified major scale.

Just for the record, the most common use of "modes" is in improvisation or soloing. Modes are used to create different tonalities against certain chords. As bass players (who are not soloing), we really have very little use for modes or modal thinking. In over 20 years of playing bass, I have had very few occasions to consider which mode I was playing in. It comes up, but very rarely. I have always found it much easier to concentrate on which scale we are drawing notes from. That is the approach I am taking in explaining these scales and modes to you in this book. If this book was about soloing, we would discuss modes in a different light. But, it's not ... so we aren't!

Anyway, here is Figure 2.3 which is the C Mixolydian scale. Figure 2.4 shows you the mixolydian scales for all twelve keys. Notice again that this is a movable fingering pattern as well.

# C Mixolydian Scale

*Fig 2.3*

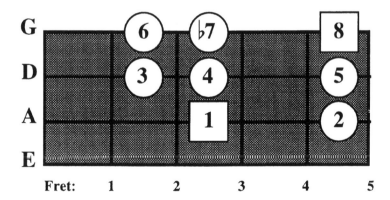

## Figure 2.4

### C Mixolydian Scale

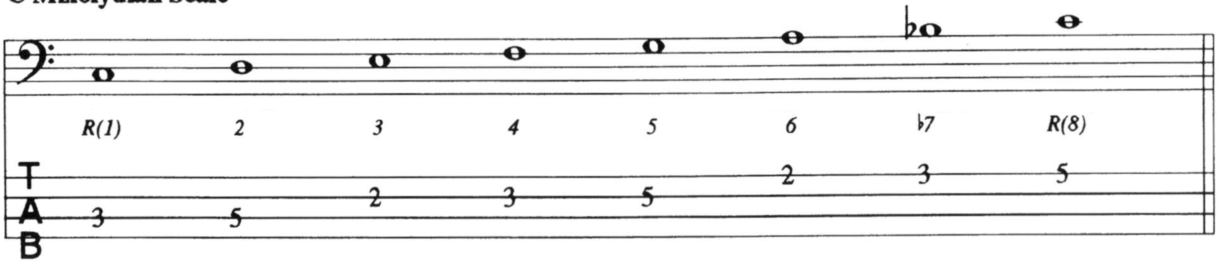

### F Mixolydian Scale

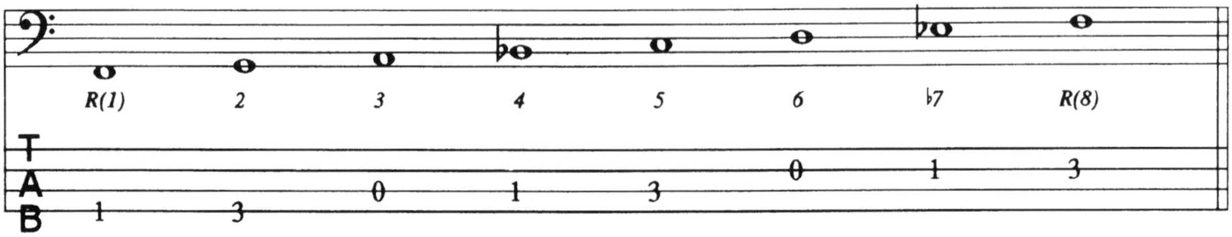

### B♭ Mixolydian Scale

### E♭ Mixolydian Scale

*Figure 2.4 (cont'd)*

**A♭ Mixolydian Scale**

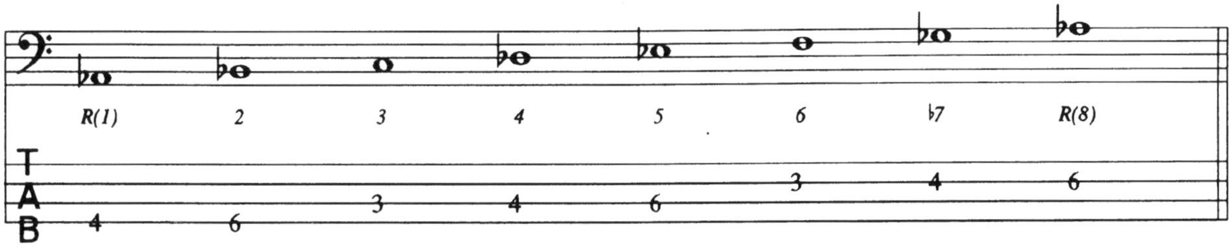

**D♭ Mixolydian Scale**

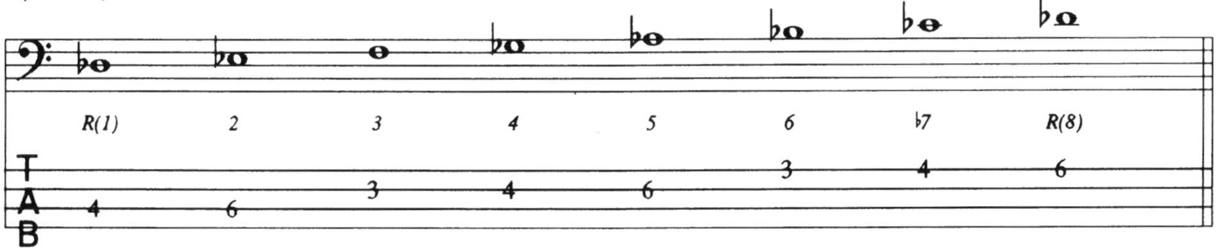

**F♯ Mixolydian Scale**

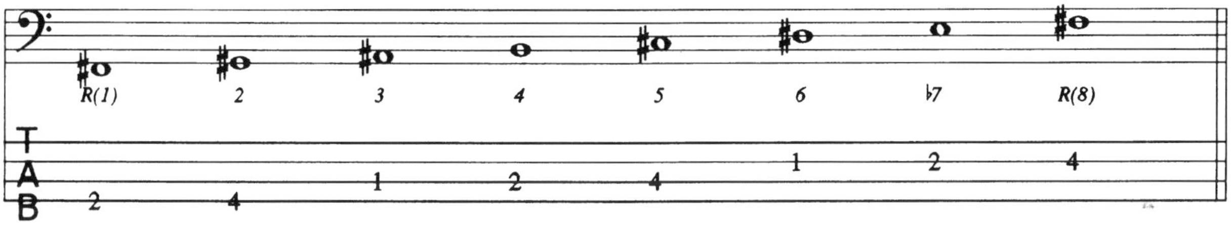

**B Mixolydian Scale**

*Figure 2.4 (cont'd)*

**E Mixolydian Scale**

**A Mixolydian Scale**

**D Mixolydian Scale**

**G Mixolydian Scale**

Exercise 2.2 shows you how to play the C Mixolydian scale in all positions up to the 12th fret. Learn it carefully, then try it with some other scales as you did with the C major scale.

*Ex 2.2*

**C Mixolydian Scale Studies**

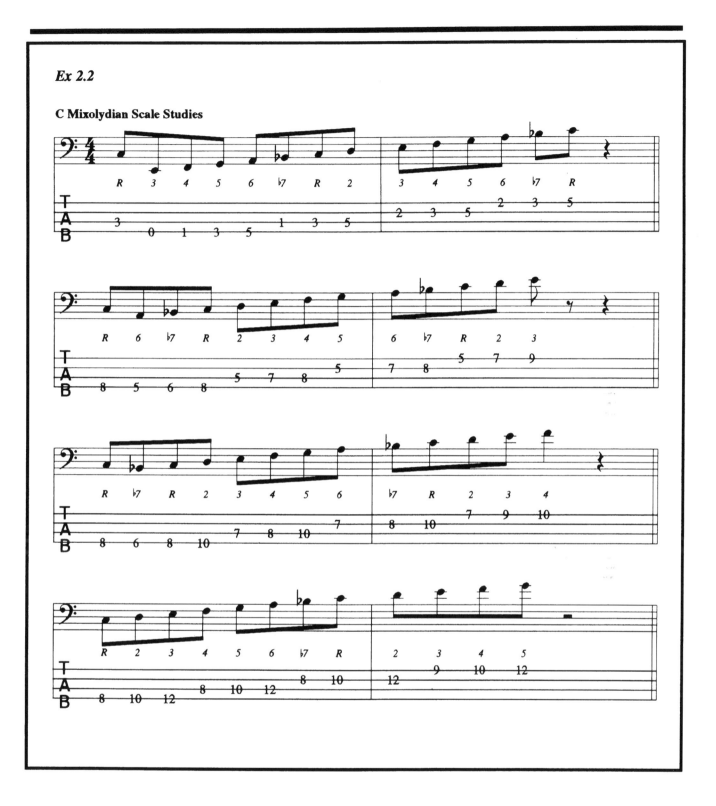

The **minor pentatonic scale** is a five-note scale based on the minor scale. Let's think of it relative to the major scale, though. It uses the root, a lowered or flat 3rd (aka minor 3rd), the 4th, 5th and flat 7th scale tones. By thinking of these scales relative to the major scale, you should still be able to "see" how the major scale falls on top of and around the notes in the minor pentatonic scale. When you can identify the major scale around the notes you are playing (even if you are not playing notes in the major scale), then you will have a very complete understanding of the notes on your fingerboard.

Figure 2.5 shows you the notes in the C minor pentatonic scale and Figure 2.6 lists all twelve of the minor pentatonic scales. Use Exercise 2.3 to learn the C minor pentatonic scale in all positions up to the 12th fret and then go learn the other eleven minor pentatonic scales using the same approach. (I know it's a lot of work, but it's better than not getting any gigs!)

# C Minor Pentatonic Scale

*Fig 2.5*

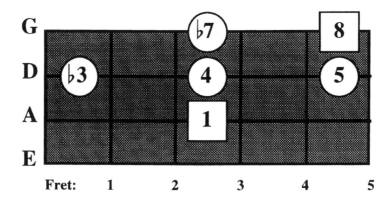

*Figure 2.6*

**C Minor Pentatonic Scale**

R(1) ♭3 4 5 ♭7 R(8)
T
A
B
3 1 3 5 3 5

**F Minor Pentatonic Scale**

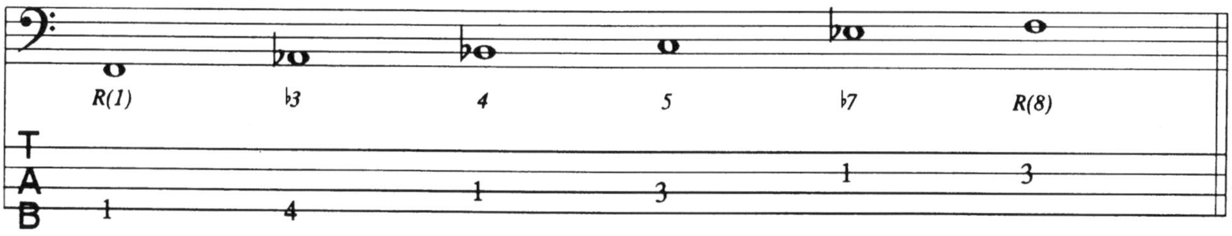
R(1) ♭3 4 5 ♭7 R(8)
T
A
B
1 4 1 3 1 3

**B♭ Minor Pentatonic Scale**

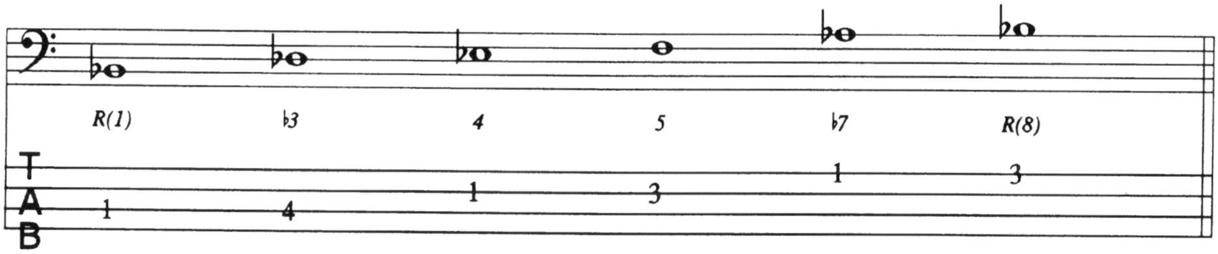
R(1) ♭3 4 5 ♭7 R(8)
T
A
B
1 4 1 3 1 3

**E♭ Minor Pentatonic Scale**

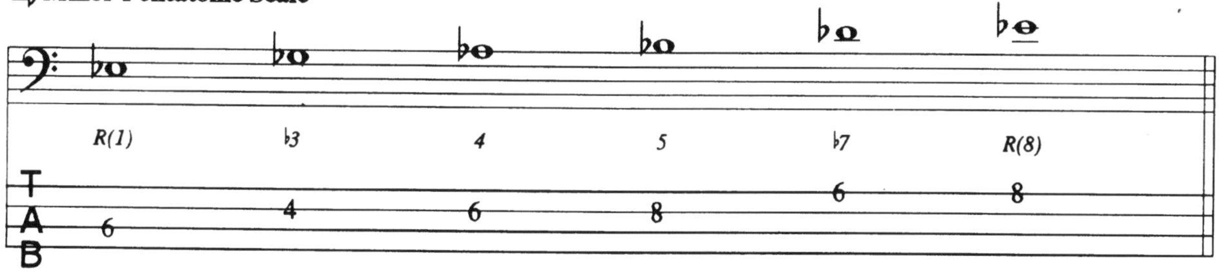
R(1) ♭3 4 5 ♭7 R(8)
T
A
B
6 4 6 8 6 8

*Figure 2.6 (cont'd)*

**A♭ Minor Pentatonic Scale**

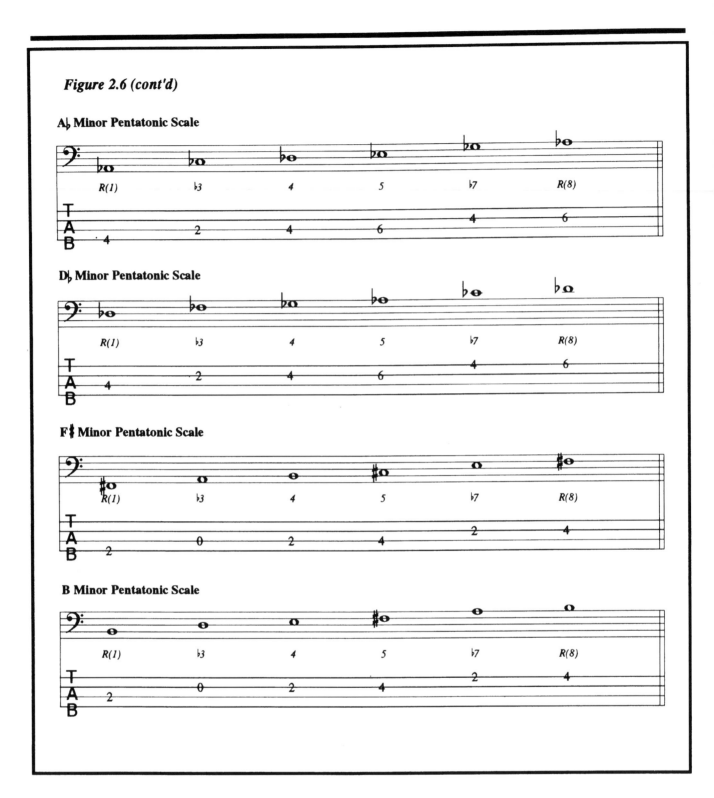

**D♭ Minor Pentatonic Scale**

**F♯ Minor Pentatonic Scale**

**B Minor Pentatonic Scale**

*Figure 2.6 (cont'd)*

**E Minor Pentatonic Scale**

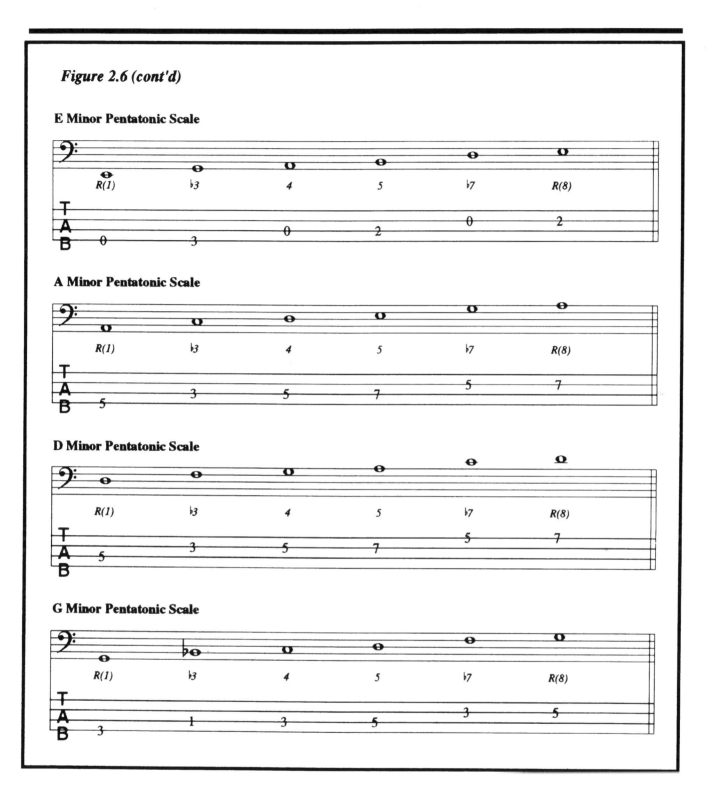

**A Minor Pentatonic Scale**

**D Minor Pentatonic Scale**

**G Minor Pentatonic Scale**

*Ex 2.3*

**C Minor Pentatonic Scale Studies**

## THE MINOR BLUES SCALE ..........................................................................................

By making a slight addition to the minor pentatonic scale, we create the **minor blues scale**. The minor blues scale contains the root, minor 3rd, 4th, lowered or flat 5th, the perfect 5th, and the flat 7th notes from the major scale. One of the things that makes the blues sound the way it does is the use of the flat 5th in fills and soloing.

As bass players, we use the flat 5th primarily as a passing tone, but because we do see some chords that are constructed using the flat 5, we need to know where it is at all times.

Figure 2.7 shows you the notes in the C minor blues scale. Figure 2.8 shows you the notes in all twelve minor blues scales, and Exercise 2.4 gives you the exercise to learn the C minor blues scale in all positions up to the 12th fret. Again, be sure to apply this exercise to all twelve minor blues scales.

# C Minor Blues Scale

*Fig 2.7*

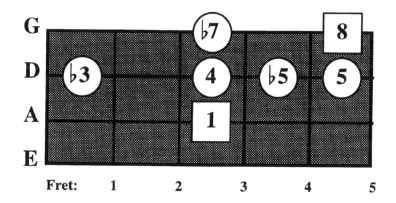

*Figure 2.8*

**C Minor Blues Scale**

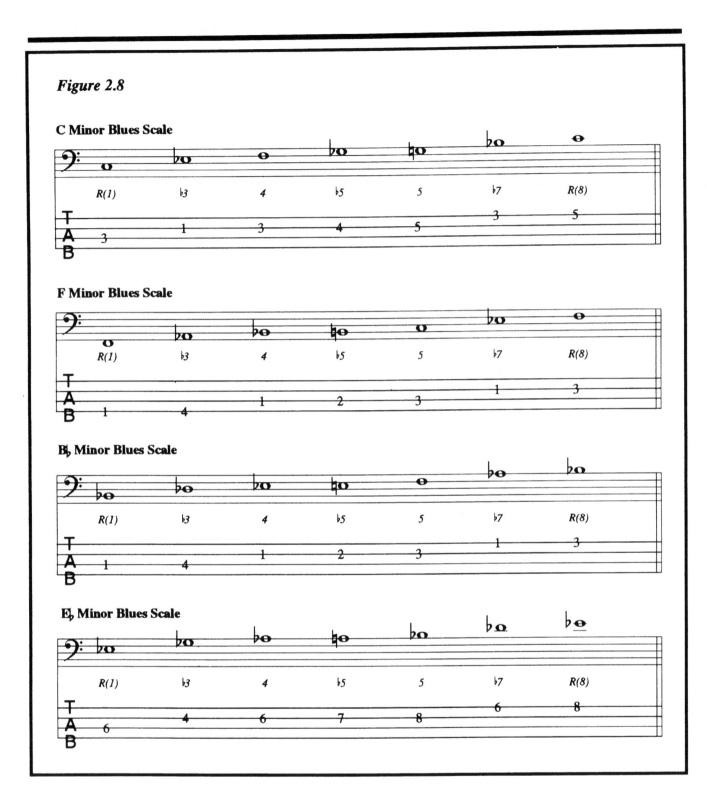

**F Minor Blues Scale**

**B♭ Minor Blues Scale**

**E♭ Minor Blues Scale**

*Figure 2.8 (cont'd)*

**A♭ Minor Blues Scale**

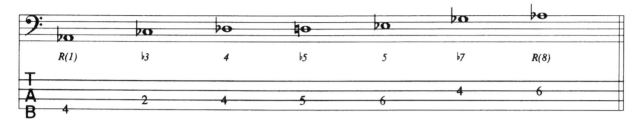

**D♭ Minor Blues Scale**

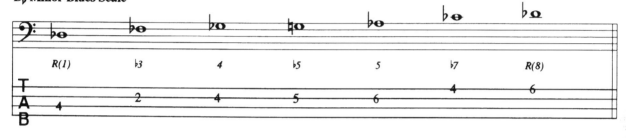

**F♯ Minor Blues Scale**

**B Minor Blues Scale**

*Figure 2.8 (cont'd)*

**E Minor Blues Scale**

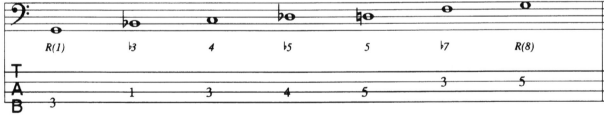

**A Minor Blues Scale**

**D Minor Blues Scale**

**G Minor Blues Scale**

*Ex 2.4*

**C Minor Blues Scale Studies**

The **altered blues scale** is the result of combining the mixolydian scale with the minor pentatonic, and minor blues scales. It is made up of all of the notes in the mixolydian scale plus the minor third and the flat 5. As you learn the blues bass lines in this book and from other sources, you will realize that the altered blues scale contains virtually all of the notes you will need. You will use some passing tones that are not in the altered blues scale, but the primary notes in your bass lines will come from this scale.

Figure 2.9 shows you the fretboard diagram for the C altered blues scale in standard position, while Figure 2.10 shows you all twelve of the altered blues scales. Exercise 2.5 shows how to play the C altered blues scale in all positions up to the 12th fret. If you want to insure that you have no social life and alienate yourself from everyone you know, go ahead and learn the altered blues scale for all twelve keys. (Actually, it's not that bad if you've learned the other scales already - Good Luck!!)

# C Altered Blues Scale

*Fig 2.9*

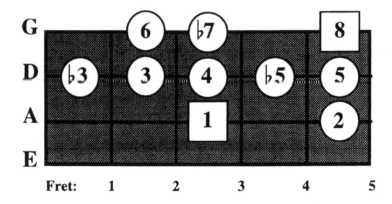

## Figure 2.10

**C Altered Blues Scale**

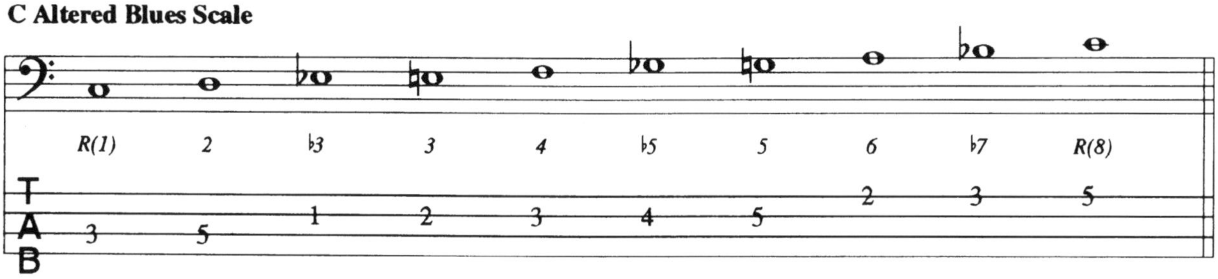

| R(1) | 2 | b3 | 3 | 4 | b5 | 5 | 6 | b7 | R(8) |
|------|---|----|----|----|----|----|----|----|------|

**F Altered Blues Scale**

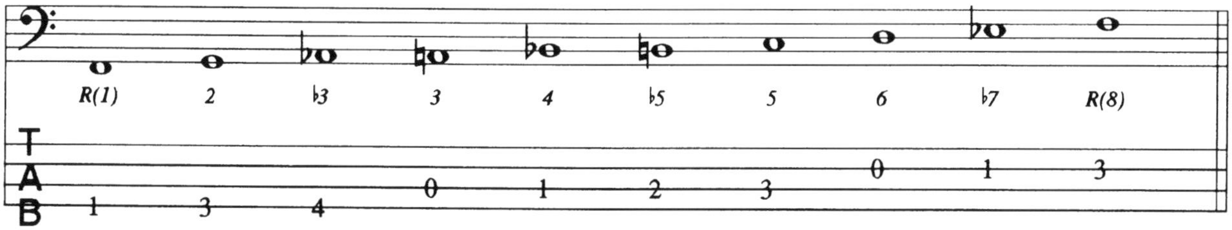

| R(1) | 2 | b3 | 3 | 4 | b5 | 5 | 6 | b7 | R(8) |
|------|---|----|----|----|----|----|----|----|------|

**Bb Altered Blues Scale**

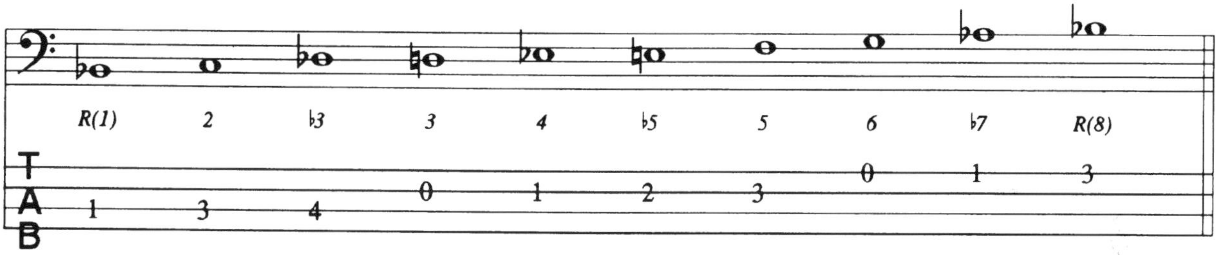

| R(1) | 2 | b3 | 3 | 4 | b5 | 5 | 6 | b7 | R(8) |
|------|---|----|----|----|----|----|----|----|------|

**Eb Altered Blues Scale**

| R(1) | 2 | b3 | 3 | 4 | b5 | 5 | 6 | b7 | R(8) |
|------|---|----|----|----|----|----|----|----|------|

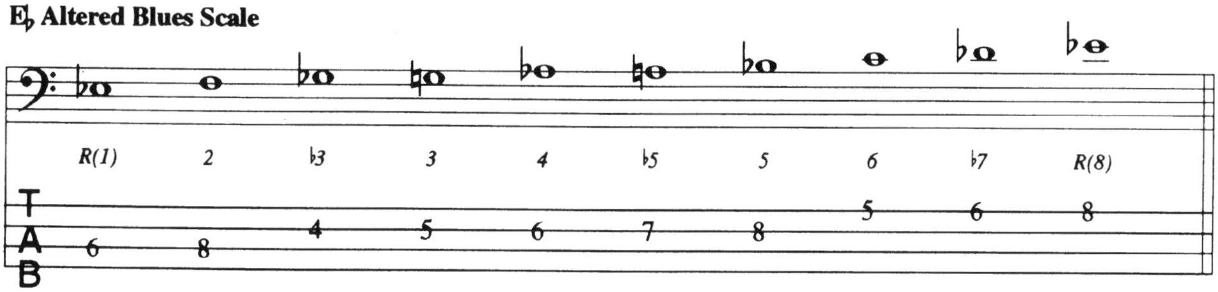

*Figure 2.10 (cont'd)*

**A♭ Altered Blues Scale**

**D♭ Altered Blues Scale**

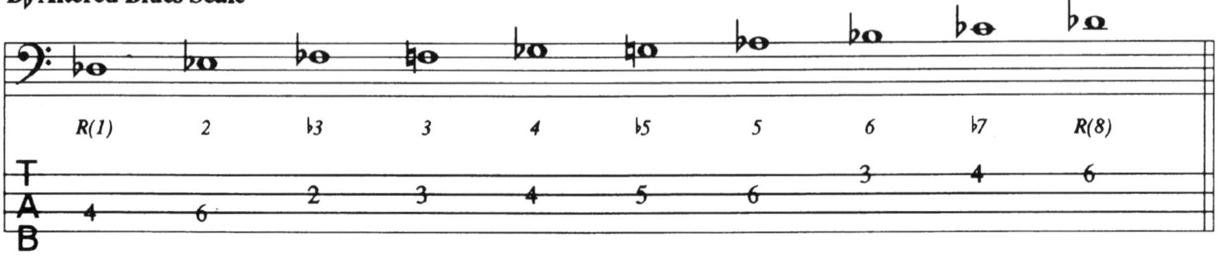

**F♯ Altered Blues Scale**

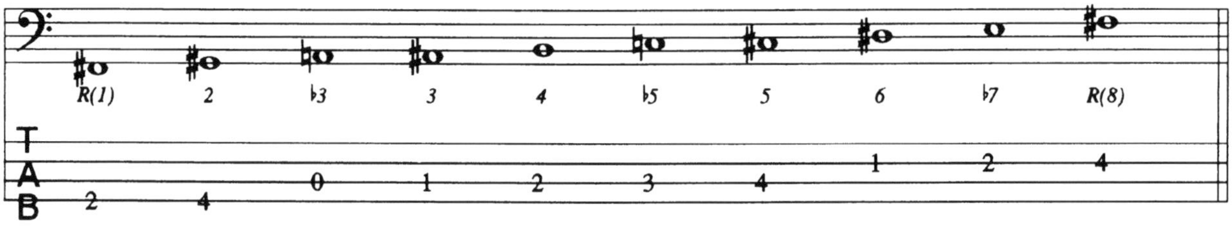

**B Altered Blues Scale**

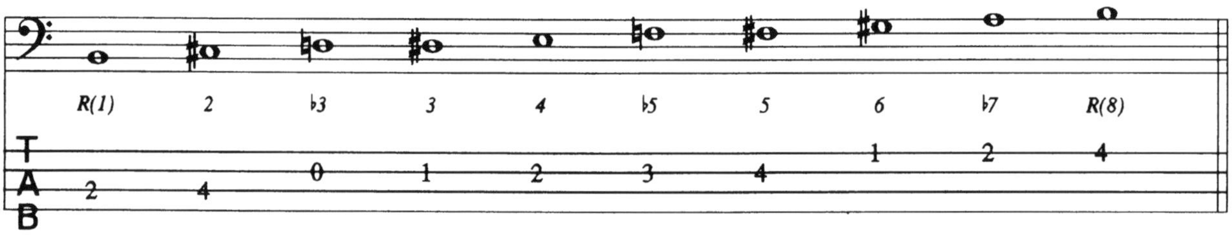

*Figure 2.10 (cont'd)*

**E Altered Blues Scale**

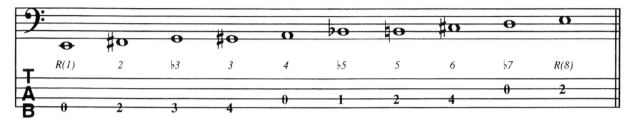

**A Altered Blues Scale**

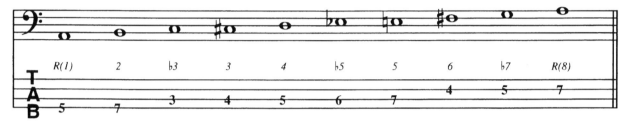

**D Altered Blues Scale**

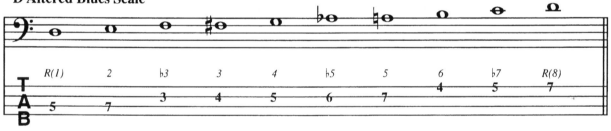

**G Altered Blues Scale**

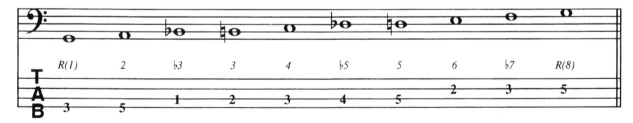

*Ex 2.5*

**C Altered Blues Scale Studies**

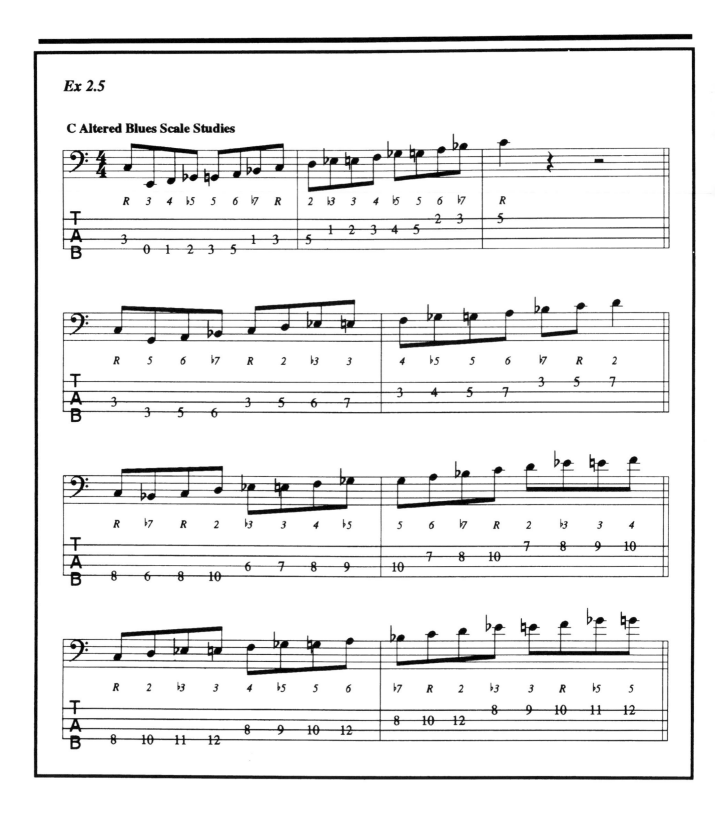

## CHORD TYPES .................................................................................................

Now that we have a firm grasp of the scales we will use in our blues bass lines (we do have that firm grasp, don't we?), let's take a look at the types of chords you are likely to see. Of course, songwriting is a very creative art form and the songwriter has the opportunity to use any old chord they please, so you may see some curveballs every once in a while. Based on our knowledge of scales, we can make some reasonable assumptions about the chord types that will be used.

The most commonly used chords are the dominant 7 chords as you learned in the first chapter. Remember that the basic 12-bar progression uses the I7, IV7, and V7 chords? Well, most blues songs consist of slight variations in the order and duration of those three chords. That's *most* of the time, not always.

As you learn about different blues styles, you will see that certain styles like to use specific chord types in specific places. This is why one style sounds different than another. The "flavors" of the chords may vary a little to create a slightly different sound. Do this a couple of times and, *viola*, a new style is born!

The first set of chord types we'll talk about are based on our major scale types, the major scale and the mixolydian scale. These two scales will supply us with our dominant 7 (and occasionally, dominant 9) chords. When you think of dominant chords, you should think of the major or mixolydian scale that is also rooted on the same note as the chord. This will enable you to find the proper chord tones more quickly.

Now, this doesn't mean that the major and mixolydian scales don't also supply us with minor chord types. I said this earlier, and it's worth repeating again; as you play a bass line under a chord, you can think of the *scale* that is rooted on the same note as the root of the chord when you are looking for notes to play against a chord.

Figure 2.11 shows you the construction of the major, dominant 7, and dominant 9 chords that we get from the major scale and mixolydian scale. You don't necessarily have to practice the notes in these chords, but it would be a good idea to memorize the chord tones that make up each chord. That would be 1, 3, 5 for major chords; 1, 3, 5, ♭7 for dominant 7 chords; and 1, 3, 5, ♭7, 9 for dominant 9 chords.

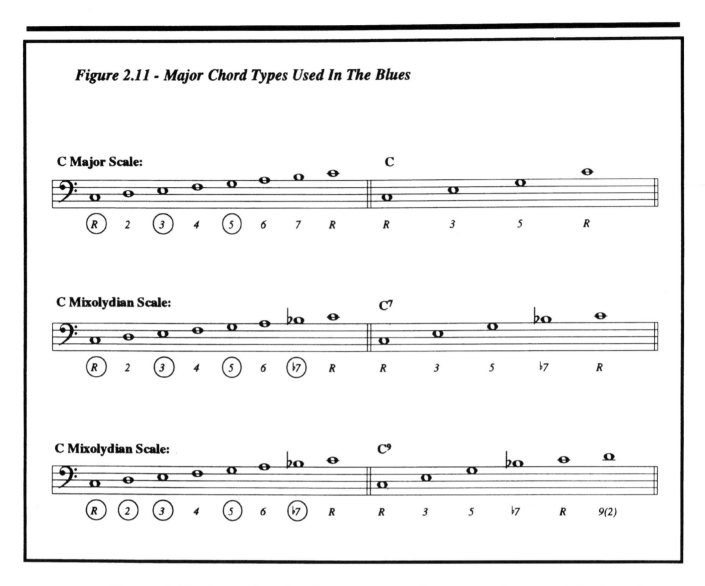

*Figure 2.11 - Major Chord Types Used In The Blues*

Figure 2.12 shows the chord types we get from our minor pentatonic and minor blues scales. So, as with the major chord types, when you see the minor chord, minor seven chord, and/or minor seven flat five chords, you can think of the minor pentatonic or minor blues scale that is rooted on the same note as the root of the chord. Again, it is a good idea to memorize the construction of these three minor chords as well.

*Figure 2.12 - Minor Chord Types Used In The Blues*

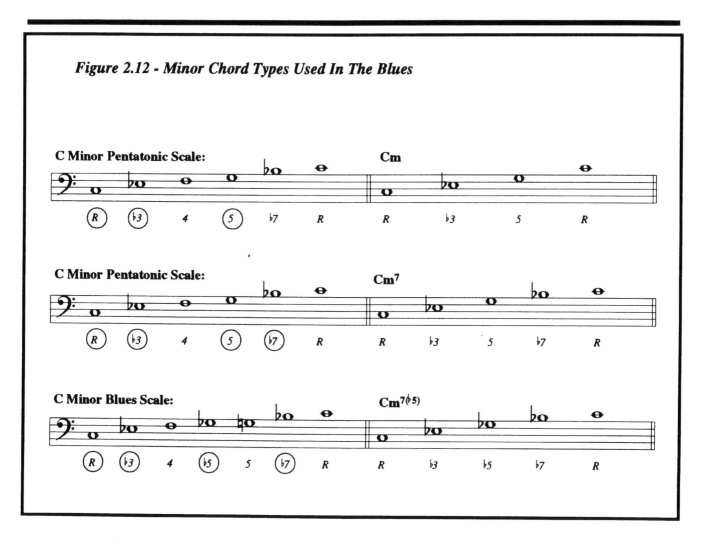

That winds up our study of scales and chords used in blues bass lines. As we go through the remaining exercises and examples, pay very close attention to the scale and chord tones used at all times. If they are indicated below the notes on the staff, then look at your fingerboard and confirm in your own mind that you know why a particular note is being called the 3rd or the 6th. Make sure you are comfortable identifying notes by their scale or chord tone numbers.

If the exercise does not have scale or chord tones identified, then figure it out! You can do this with bass lines that you already know as well. Every bass line you learn, you should analyze it this way so that you understand what you are playing. This is how we steal each other's bass lines!! Learn a part or make one up, analyze it by figuring out the scale or chord tones involved and then remember that information. Later on, when you're searching for ideas, go back in your memory (aka your "library of licks") and find one that sort of works. Change whatever is necessary to make the part fit your new application and go with it. This is how we all learn to create our own bass parts. And this form of stealing is absolutely legal!

# Blues Progressions

## BASIC 12-BAR PROGRESSIONS ................................................................

     As I said in the first chapter, there is a basic 12-bar blues progression that almost all blues songs are based on. As a reference point, Table 3.1 shows the I7, IV7, and V7 chords for all twelve keys. At this point it would be advisable to take the major walking pattern and mixolydian walking pattern described in chapter 1 and practice them in all twelve keys as specified in Table 3.1.

     If you really want to feel that you have a firm grasp of how to play the blues, at a minimum you must be able to play the basic 12-bar blues progression using these two walking patterns in any key at the drop of a hat. That progression and those walking patterns are the foundation for everything else you will play when playing the blues.

---

*Table 3.1*

# I-IV-V Chords for All Keys

**(Key)**

| I7 | IV7 | V7 |
|----|-----|----|
| C7 | F7 | G7 |
| F7 | B♭7 | C7 |
| B♭7 | E♭7 | F7 |
| E♭7 | A♭7 | B♭7 |
| A♭7 | D♭7 | E♭7 |
| D♭7 | G♭7 | A♭7 |
| F♯7 | B7 | C♯7 |
| B7 | E7 | F♯7 |
| E7 | A7 | B7 |
| A7 | D7 | E7 |
| D7 | G7 | A7 |
| G7 | C7 | D7 |

---

At this point we will start looking at some of the common variations on the basic 12-bar blues chord progression. All of these variations use the I7, IV7, and V7 chords as we have discussed so far. A couple of the variations will also use the iim7 chord in addition to the other three. (Remember, that is the "two-minor-seven" chord: lower case Roman Numerals indicate minor chords.) The use of the iim7 chord comes into play when we talk about a style called "jump blues". We'll see this more in depth in the next chapter. But, it is a common enough variation to be included at this point.

Table 3.2 shows seven different variations on the basic blues progression (which is included as the first entry in the table). Use this table for reference only at this point, we'll see some musical examples of these progressions in a moment. Note that "I7/V7" means that the I7 chord is played during beats 1 & 2, and then the V7 chord is played for beats 3 & 4 of the indicated measure.

*Table 3.2*

# 12-Bar Blues Progressions

| Measure Number: | 1 | 2 | 3 | 4 | 5 | 6 | 7 | 8 | 9 | 10 | 11 | 12 |
|---|---|---|---|---|---|---|---|---|---|---|---|---|
| **Chord:** | I7 | I7 | I7 | I7 | IV7 | IV7 | I7 | I7 | V7 | V7 | I7 | I7 |
| | I7 | I7 | I7 | I7 | IV7 | IV7 | I7 | I7 | V7 | IV7 | I7 | I7 |
| | I7 | I7 | I7 | I7 | IV7 | IV7 | I7 | I7 | V7 | IV7 | I7 | I7/V7 |
| | I7 | IV7 | I7 | I7 | IV7 | IV7 | I7 | I7 | V7 | IV7 | I7 | I7/V7 |
| | I7 | IV7 | I7 | I7 | IV7 | IV7 | I7 | I7 | V7 | IV7 | I7 | V7 |
| | I7 | I7 | I7 | I7 | IV7 | IV7 | I7 | I7 | iim7 | V7 | I7 | I7 |
| | I7 | IV7 | I7 | I7 | IV7 | IV7 | I7 | I7 | iim7 | V7 | I7 | I7 |

Exercises 3.1 through 3.6 are musical examples of some of these new variations in action. Pay close attention to the chord tones indicated below each note. From this point on, if a chord tone is indicated as a "P", that means it is a passing tone. A passing tone is a note that it not part of the current chord (or scale) and is being used like a "stepping stone" to get from one chord tone to another or from one chord to the next chord. Sometimes passing tones may be interpreted as a scale or chord tone, but if I have indicated it as a passing tone, it's because that's how I want you to think about it for that particular exercise. Be sure to play each exercise a couple of times to insure that you understand the progression and why each one is different from the others.

**Ex 3.1**

*Ex 3.2*

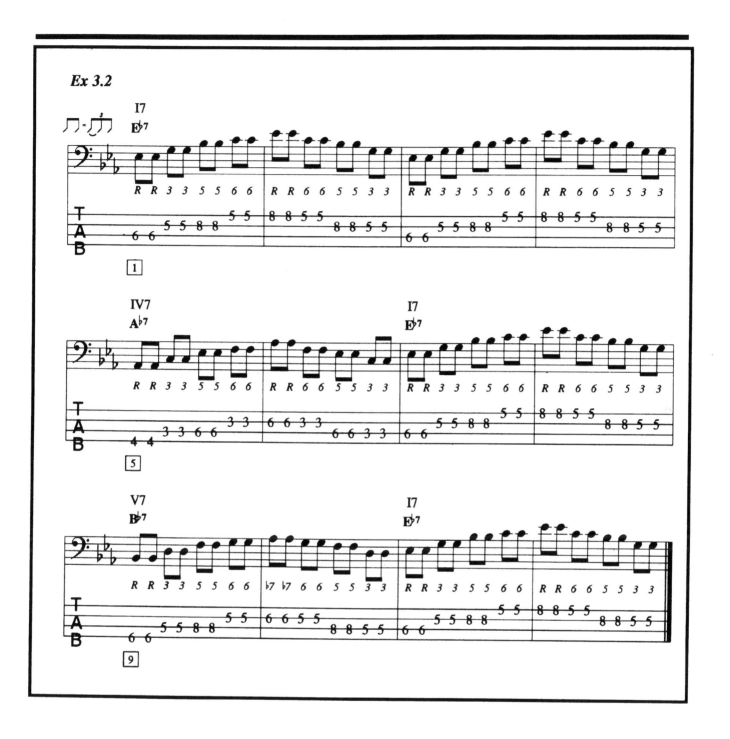

**Ex 3.3**

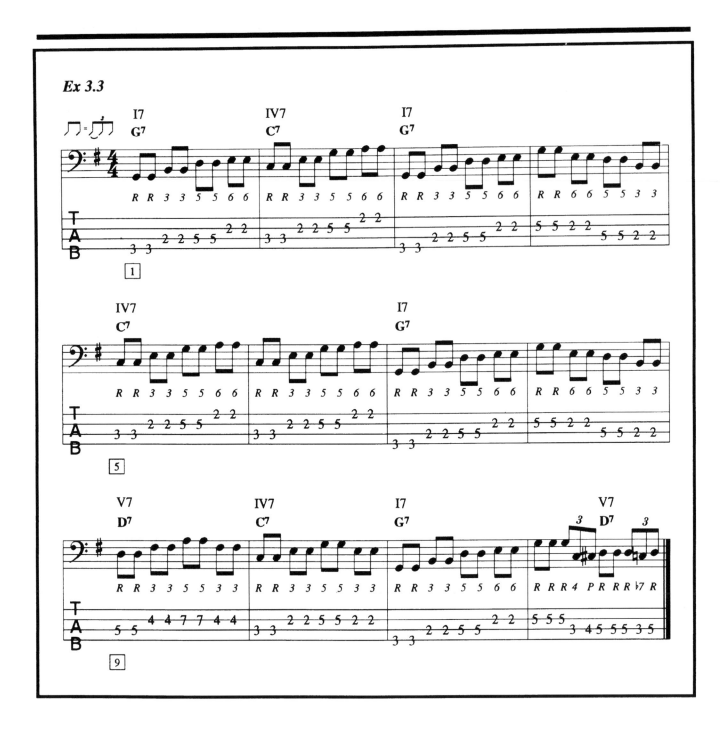

**Ex 3.4**

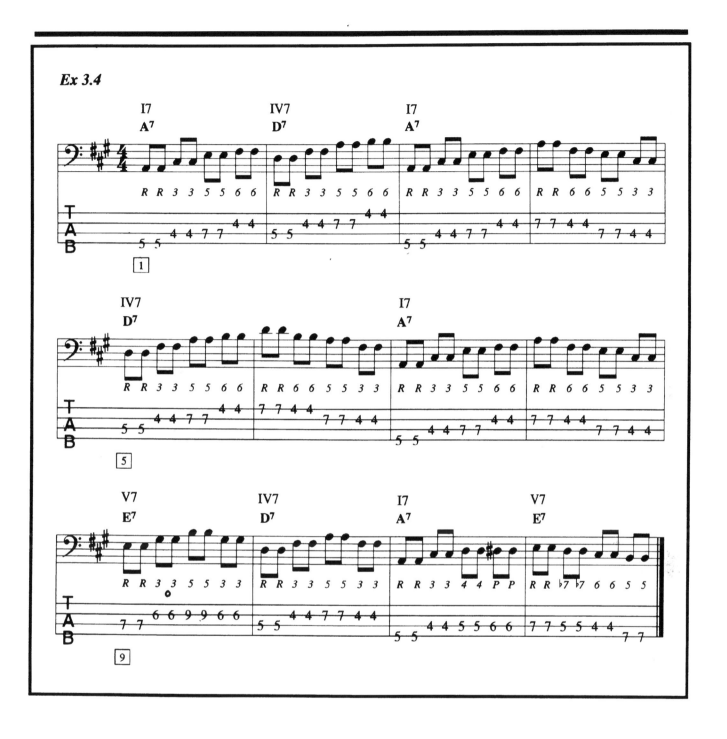

**Ex 3.5**

**\*NOTE:** "P/O" means "pull-off" with the left-hand to the following note.

**Ex 3.6**

Another fairly common blues progression is only eight bars long. This, obviously, would be referred to as an 8-bar blues progression. There are four variations that are pretty common. The possibilities are not limited to these four, but these are definitely the ones you will encounter most often. Table 3.3 shows you those four variations of the 8-bar blues progression. Exercises 3.7 through 3.11 are examples of 8-bar blues progressions.

*Table 3.3*

# 8-Bar Blues Progressions

| Measure Number: | 1 | 2 | 3 | 4 | 5 | 6 | 7 | 8 |
|---|---|---|---|---|---|---|---|---|
| **Chord:** | I7 | I7 | IV7 | IV7 | V7 | V7 | I7 | I7 |
| | I7 | V7 | IV7 | IV7 | I7 | IV7 | I7/IV7 | I7/V7 |
| | IV7 | IV7 | I7 | I7 | V7 | IV7 | I7 | I7 |
| | IV7 | IV7 | I7 | I7 | V7 | V7 | I7 | I7 |

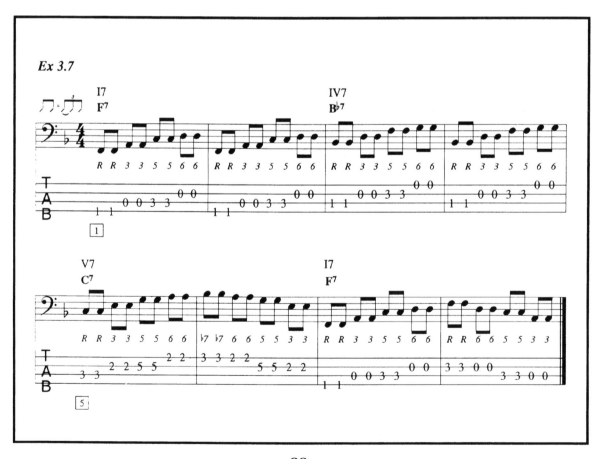

*Ex 3.7*

**Ex 3.8**

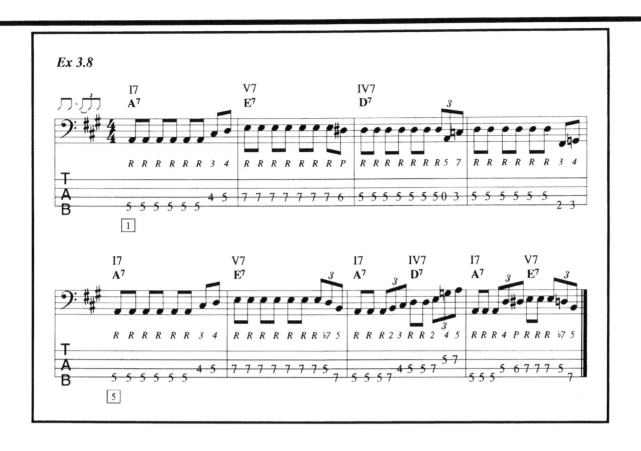

**Ex 3.9**

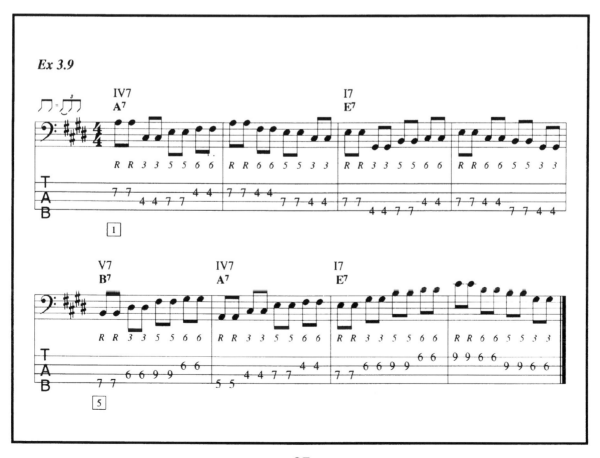

*Ex 3.10*

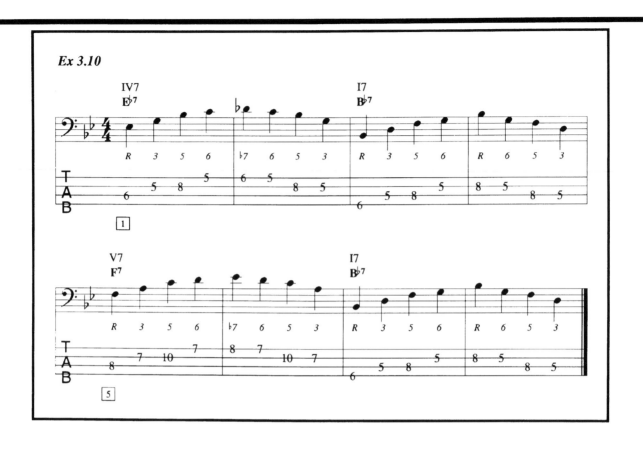

*Ex 3.11*

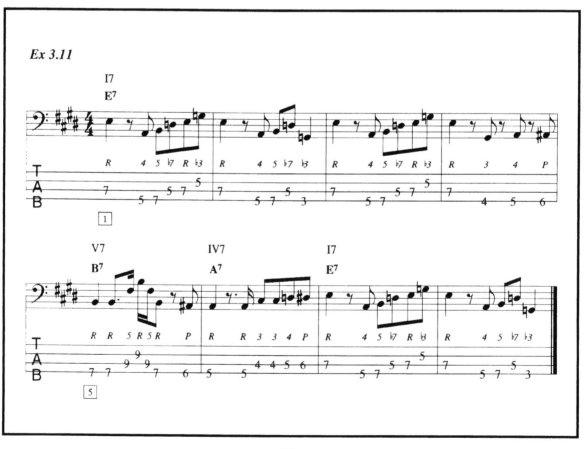

Occasionally, you will come up against a 16-bar blues progression. They are far more rare than the 12-bar or 8-bar progressions and there are typically not too many variations. We will just look at one 16-bar blues progression.

On a side note, many times in a 16-bar progression, the first four bars of the verse would just be the I7 chord and then, starting at bar 5, one of the normal 12-bar progressions would begin. (I don't have a calculator handy, but I'm pretty sure that adds up to 16 bars.....)

Table 3.4 shows you an example of a 16-bar blues progression, and Exercise 3.12 is a musical example of the same progression.

---

*Table 3.4*

# 16-Bar Blues Progression

**Measure Number:**

| 1 | 2 | 3 | 4 | 5 | 6 | 7 | 8 | 9 | 10 | 11 | 12 | 13 | 14 | 15 | 16 |
|---|---|---|---|---|---|---|---|---|----|----|----|----|----|----|----|

**Chord:**

| I7 | I7 | I7 | I7 | I7 | I7 | V7 | V7 | I7 | I7 | IV7 | IV7 | I7 | V7 | I7 | V7 |

---

*Ex 3.12*

## MINOR BLUES PROGRESSIONS ...............................................................................

The final type of blues progression we are going to talk about is the minor blues progression. This means that the chords are based on a minor key instead of a major key. In minor blues progressions, you typically find that the one and four chords are minor seven chords (im7 and ivm7, respectively) and the five chord is a dominant 7 (V7). The 12-bar progression is usually similar to one of the basic 12-bar progressions we looked at earlier in this chapter. The only exception to this is that many minor blues songs make use of the VI chord. Now, the sixth scale tone is only one half-step above the fifth scale tone, making it a flat six (or minor six). When you are talking about minor keys and minor progressions, the six chord may be referred to as either the "six" or the "minor six" chord. This does not mean that the six chord is a minor chord, rather that it is the minor six to the key. The six chord is also a major chord and is sometimes played without adding a 7th. So, the six chord can be a basic major chord (root, 3rd, 5th) or a dominant 7 chord. Because it is major, the Roman Numeral is "VI" in our musical examples.

Many times when playing minor blues progressions, you will find that the V7 chord is substituted with an altered chord. Usually it is the V7($\flat$9) or V7($\sharp$9). This means that a flat nine or sharp nine is added on top of the root, 3rd, 5th, and $\flat$7 chord tones. When you are playing walking blues bass lines, you really aren't concerned with such alterations. Your job is to establish the foundation of the chord, that is the root, 3rd, 5th, and/or $\flat$7th. Leave the harmonic embellishments to the guitar and piano players. Concentrate on the groove, not the frilly little notes hanging off the top of some altered chord.

OK, enough about that. Table 3.5 shows you three variations of minor blues progressions. Exercises 3.13, 3.14, and 3.15 are examples of bass lines you might play under a minor blues. Notice that there is very little use of the minor third in the bass lines. Due to the "mood" created by minor chords, it is usually best to stick to the root, 5th, and $\flat$7th. Typical walking bass lines can sound a little weaker against some minor blues progressions. You can't go wrong with the root, 5th, and $\flat$7th.

*Table 3.5*

# Minor Blues Progressions

| Measure Number: | 1 | 2 | 3 | 4 | 5 | 6 | 7 | 8 | 9 | 10 | 11 | 12 |
|---|---|---|---|---|---|---|---|---|---|---|---|---|
| **Chord:** | im7 | im7 | im7 | im7 | ivm7 | ivm7 | im7 | im7 | V7 | V7 | im7 | im7 |
| | im7 | ivm7 | im7 | im7 | ivm7 | ivm7 | im7 | im7 | V7 | ivm7 | im7 | iim7/V7 |
| | im7 | im7 | im7 | im7 | ivm7 | ivm7 | im7 | im7 | VI | V7 | im7 | im7 |

*Ex 3.13*

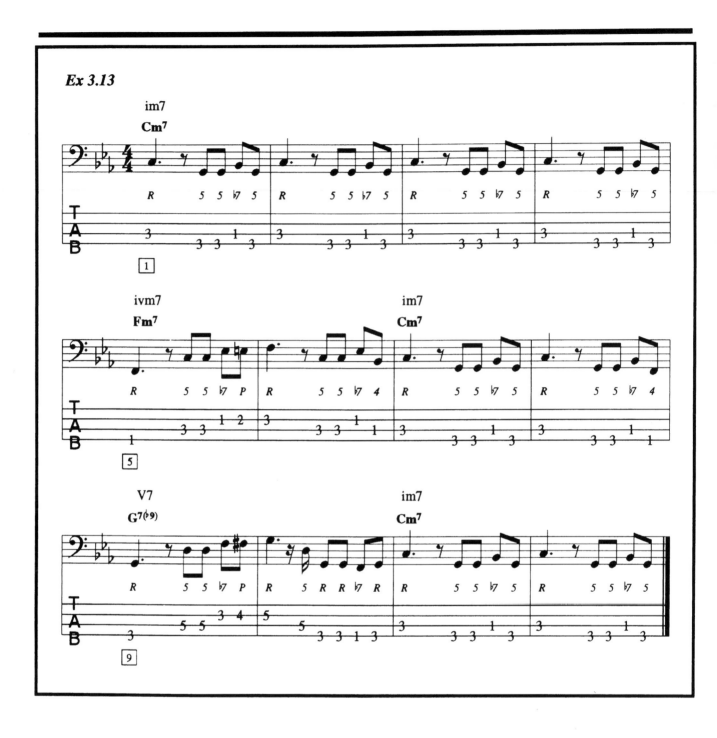

*Ex 3.14*

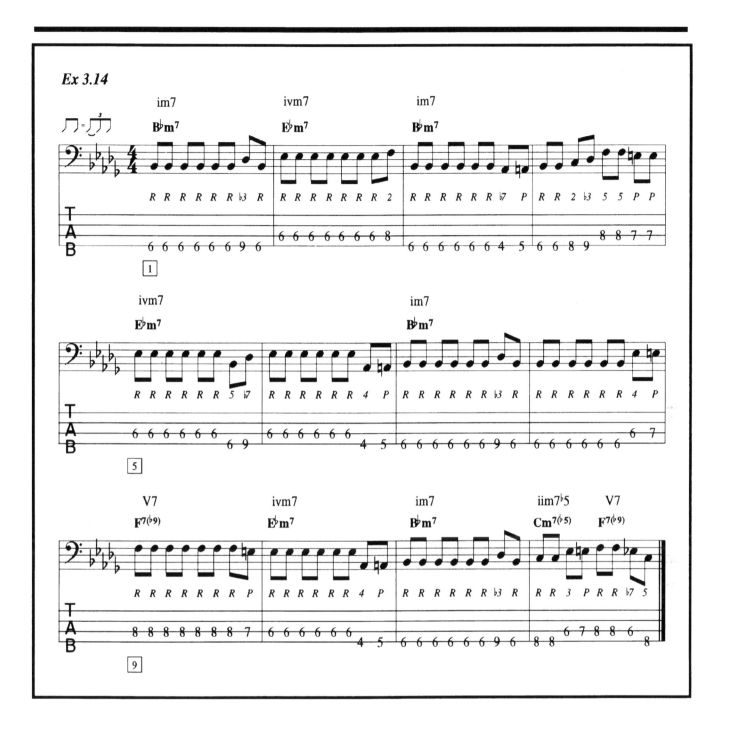

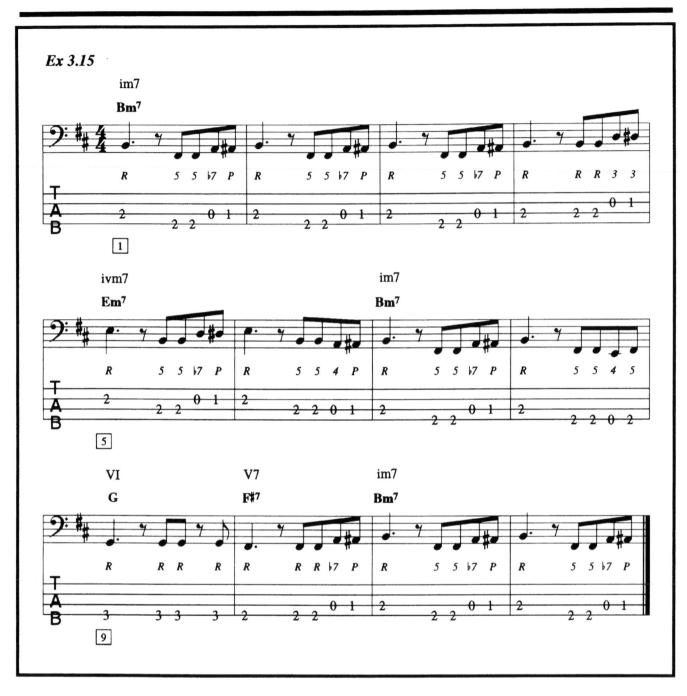

**Ex 3.15**

Let's recap what we've done so far. We now know that there is a basic 12-bar blues progression that most blues songs follow. By making a few changes, we can create a large number of possible blues progressions. There are also 8-bar and 16-bar blues progressions as well as those that are based on minor keys. Against the chords in these progressions, we are going to play selected chord tones and add a few "passing" tones to get us from one chord to the next (or from one *chord tone* to the next). If you start with your basic major scale and mixolydian walking patterns, you can then add a few extra notes for continuity to create more fluid walking lines, creating smooth transitions between chords. In a nutshell, you can play the blues! The next thing to do is a little history lesson. In the next chapter we start looking at some of the different *styles* of blues music and how your bass lines help create that style.

# Blues Styles

It is not my intention to provide a history of the blues as a lead-in to this chapter, which will provide you with and explain a number of different blues "styles". Instead, I want to present these styles with some analysis so you will understand what makes a certain style sound different than another.

The difficulty comes in that because styles evolve from other styles, they will usually appear very similar, or overlap in a number of areas. The point of this chapter is to expose you to a number of different approaches to playing the blues, the outcome of which should provide you with the basic understanding you will need to play virtually any style of the blues you desire.

By most accounts, the blues originated on the many plantations in the south in the early 1900's. These early blues sounds are commonly referred to nowadays as the "Mississippi Delta" sound. As artists began to roam the country and play their music in other cities, this style began to change somewhat. This is why some blues styles are associated with a specific city or state (i.e. Chicago Blues, Texas Blues, St. Louis Blues, etc...). And this is also why some artists are associated with those specific styles. They were the artists creating these styles based on their experiences in those cities.

This also brings us to another point of confusion. While Stevie Ray Vaughan was from Texas and certainly played a style of Texas Blues, he also played and incorporated elements of many other styles as well. This is because of how those other artists and styles influenced him in his development as a musician. As we learn to play different styles and learn things from different players, we incorporate all of those influences into our own style. Now you can see why it is so hard to put labels on musical styles and artists. They don't always exactly fit the label.

The moral of the story is, as you go through this and other books you should refer to the musical styles and artists that may be mentioned, but keep in mind that none of those references are exclusive to that particular style or artist. I've seen Buddy Guy play some very, very convincing Texas Blues, and he is primarily considered a Chicago Blues artist!!

Again, this chapter's purpose is to expose you to a number of different blues styles so that you can apply them as necessary in your own playing. You will find that many times, no one actually says to play a "Texas swing" and you are left to experiment with different patterns and styles until the right one fits. This is where having a library of ideas to pull from comes in handy. So, here goes....

As I mentioned earlier, the blues started to come to life in the early 1900's. In case you didn't know, the electric bass guitar wasn't born until around 1951. Before the electric bass guitar came into the picture, upright basses were used. Now, most musicians were pretty poor (as we still are!) and couldn't always afford an upright bass. Many times other "bass" instruments were used. Early blues bass lines were often very "Tuba"-like. That is, they were root-fifth bass patterns following the chord progressions. Figure 4.1 shows you an example of an original Tuba bass part as played through a basic 12-bar blues progression in the key of C.

**Fig 4.1**

**Original "Tuba" Bass Part**

As we go through this chapter, and the remainder of this book, you should notice just how many blues bass lines and patterns will stick with this root-fifth pattern. What I mean by that is that the root is played on the first beat of the measure and the fifth is played on the third beat. This follows a concept used in walking bass lines called *"strong beat/weak beat"*. The strong beats are one and three, and the weak beats are two and four. The idea is to play chord tones on strong beats and passing tones on the weak beats. In walking blues bass lines most of the notes we play are chord tones, so we imply the strong beats by playing the *strongest* chord tones (root and fifth) on those beats.

If you think back to the major and mixolydian walking patterns we learned earlier, you'll find that they typically conform (except that in the mixolydian pattern, the ♭7th is used on the first beat when the pattern begins to walk back down to the lower octave of the root). Keep this strong beat/weak beat concept in mind when reviewing the bass lines in this book as well as when you go to make up your own.

**TEXAS SWING** ...........................................................................................................................

As the blues migrated into Texas, it was mixed with the styles that were popular in Texas at the time which consisted of country, folk, creole, cajun, and a few years later, country swing. As this happened, the bass parts (which were often played on upright bass and doubled on piano from time to time) followed the root-fifth tuba pattern. As time went by, they began to add the use of the major 3rd chord tone to provide movement between chords. This style is often referred to as **Texas Swing**. Exercise 4.1 is an example of an early Texas swing blues bass line.

Exercises 4.2 and 4.3 show how the bass lines continued to progress using the major 3rd and eventually adding the sixth into the pattern. Notice that in virtually every bar, the root is still played on the first beat and the fifth is played on the third beat.

**Texas Swing**

T-Bone Walker popularized a style of guitar playing that eventually led to the "walking" bass lines that we know and love today. Exercises 4.4 and 4.5 are examples of this style of Texas swing as recorded by artists such as T-Bone Walker and Pee Wee Crayton. Many times, these bass lines and arrangements were played in a "big-band" type setting, complete with horns and piano. The piano would often double the bass line (as would the guitar) to bring out the driving rhythm of the walking bass pattern.

# Uptempo Texas Walk

The **Texas Shuffle** eventually evolved out of these types of walking patterns. While the walking Texas swing bass lines are often based on the major walking pattern, the Texas shuffle bass lines usually look like some form of the mixolydian walking pattern, taking advantage of the ♭7th to emphasize that "dominant" sound that has become to signify the blues. The Texas shuffle is usually a triplet feel and will most often be written as eighth notes for ease of reading.

Exercises 4.6, 4.7, and 4.8 are examples of common Texas shuffle walking bass lines.

# Texas Shuffle

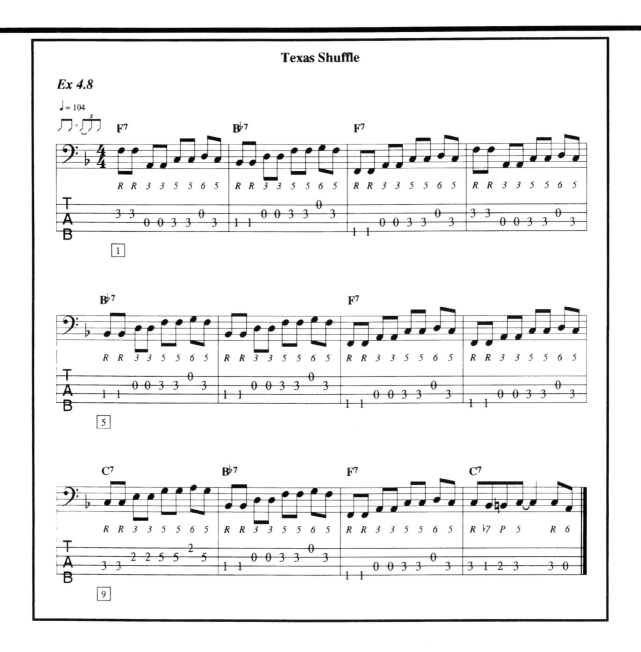

**Texas Shuffle**

*Ex 4.8*

These are just a few examples of Texas blues bass lines, but they represent a good starting point. As we go through the rest of this book you will find other examples of Texas blues progressions, bass lines, turnarounds and fills. Recommended listening to understand the history of Texas blues would include such artists as Blind Lemon Jefferson, Lightnin' Hopkins, T-Bone Walker, Pee Wee Crayton, Albert Collins, The Fabulous Thunderbirds, and Stevie Ray Vaughan and Double Trouble.

"Jumping the blues" evolved out of the Kansas City and St. Louis areas when traditionally jazz big bands began to incorporate the simpler arrangements of blues and ragtime into the powerful drive at the heart of the big band sound. **Jump blues** as it is commonly called, is primarily dance music and some of the classic jump tunes actually have been redone by other artists with great success. Ever hear of a kid named Elvis Presley? One of his early hits was a song called "Hound Dog", which was recorded in 1952 by Big Mama Thornton as a jump blues song. Elvis sold a few more copies, but it wasn't the first time that song was on the charts!

Exercises 4.9, 4.10, 4.11, and 4.12 are examples of jump blues bass lines. Jump blues bass lines are typically all quarter notes and make use of dead notes, dead note pull-offs, and open-string pull-offs (all of which are also upright bass techniques used by many jazz bassists) to create movement in the groove. These additional notes and dead notes add a certain "jump" to the rhythm. The quarter note pattern may also be doubled by the piano in many songs.

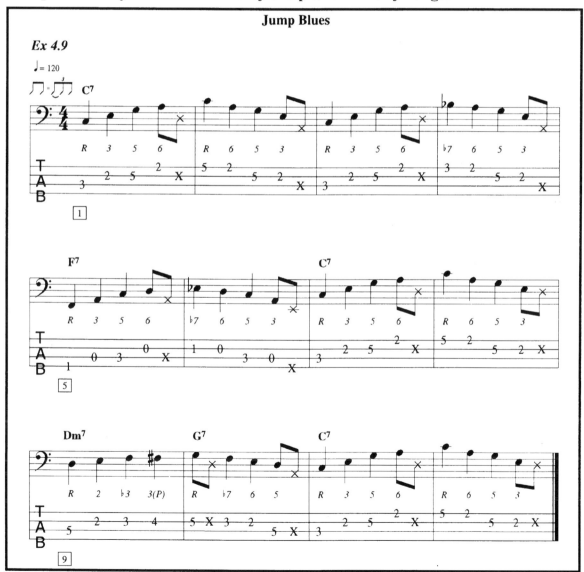

**Jump Blues**

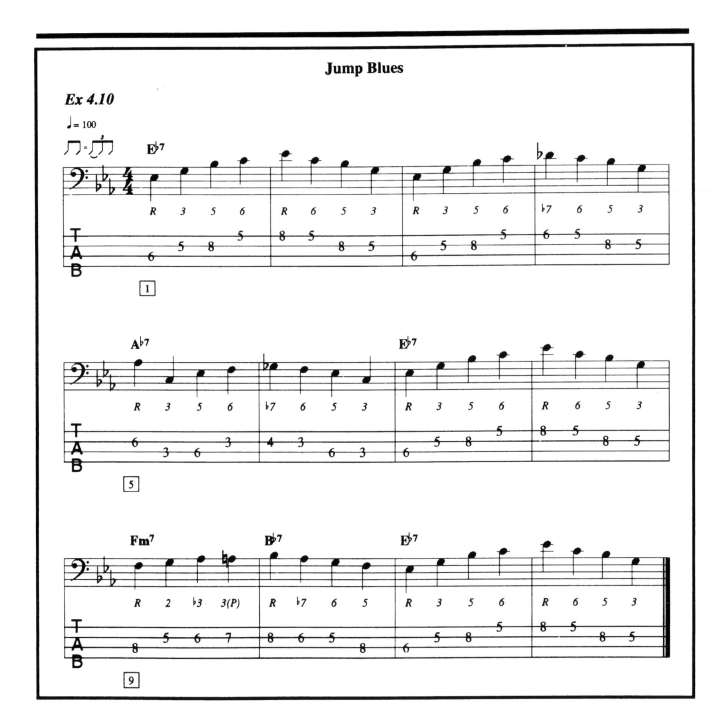

# Jump Blues

**Ex 4.11**

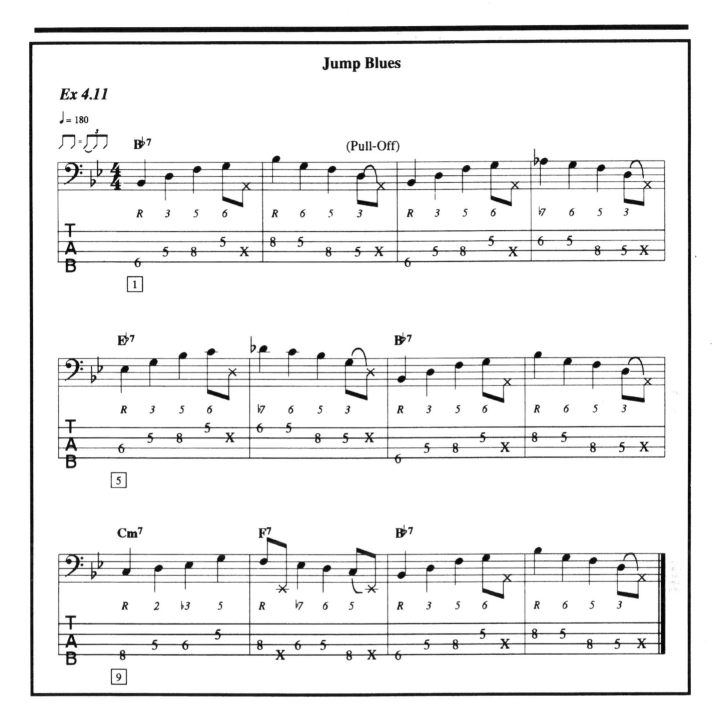

## Jump Blues

*Ex 4.12*

$\quad$ = 144

If you listen to just a few jump blues tunes by the likes of Big Joe Turner, Red Prysock, Louis Prima, and Roy Brown you will immediately understand why rock 'n roll and the blues are so closely related. To put it simply, early rock 'n roll sounds an awful lot like jumping the blues in many instances.

## CHICAGO BLUES ........................................................................................................................

With the increasing popularity of electric guitars came the popularity of amplifiers for those guitars (naturally!). **Chicago blues** as we have come to know it grew out of this rather unsurprising statement. Chicago as a city is said to be tough, fast, loud, and hard. This is reflected in the style of blues that bears the city's name.

Artists such as Muddy Waters, Howlin' Wolf, Otis Rush, and Buddy Guy are no strangers to the volume control, nor to the popular style known as Chicago blues. The interesting thing is that most artists associated with the Chicago blues style are not from Chicago. They come from various places in the south, where they learned to play the blues from the long line of Mississippi Delta greats. Somehow, they all managed to land in Chicago and mix their knowledge of the blues with the heartbeat of the city resulting in a style that is undoubtedly the blues, but with a much louder, faster, and harder edge to it.

As a bassist, you will find many of the same types of walking patterns as Texas blues and even Jump blues styles already discussed. Chicago blues tends to lean more heavily on the mixolydian patterns due to the unmistakable "bluesy" sound created by the dominant 7th at higher volumes. You also find some more interesting rhythmic patterns due to the fact that when the guitars get louder, the drummers hit harder, meaning that the rhythm section starts to create a more driving, pounding groove.

Exercises 4.13, 4.14, and 4.15 are examples of Chicago blues bass lines from the likes of Otis Rush, Buddy Guy and Muddy Waters. In Ex. 4.15, note the use of the ♭7 chord tone on the third beat, which is a strong beat, to really emphasize the dominant seven sound.

Exercise 4.16 is an example of how Junior Wells was able to combine elements of the Chicago blues sound with funk figures to create what would be considered a rhythm and blues (R&B) groove. This is done rhythmically through the use of the sixteenth-note/eighth-note combination in beat three. Be sure to notice that this bass line consists solely of the root, fifth, and flat seven (1, 5, ♭7) chord tones. Most R&B bass lines rely heavily on these three chord tones.

**Chicago Blues**

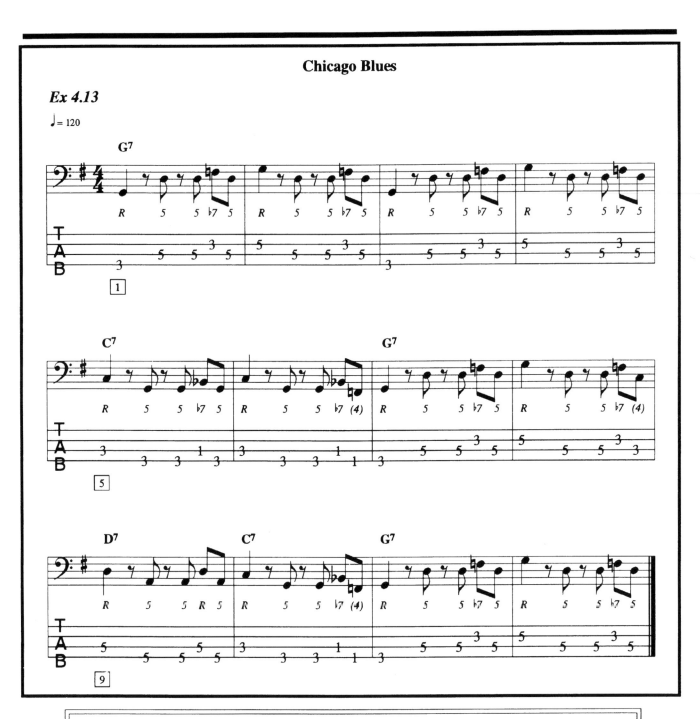

**NOTE:** The last note in measures 6, 8, and 10 are the "4" to the current chord, but they are also "♭7" to the next chord. Using the ♭7 in this manner helps to *imply* the next chord. When the chord is played (on the downbeat of measures 7, 9, and 11), the ♭7 resolves to the chord. This produces a very solid "bluesy" passage from one chord to the next.

# Muddy Waters Shuffle

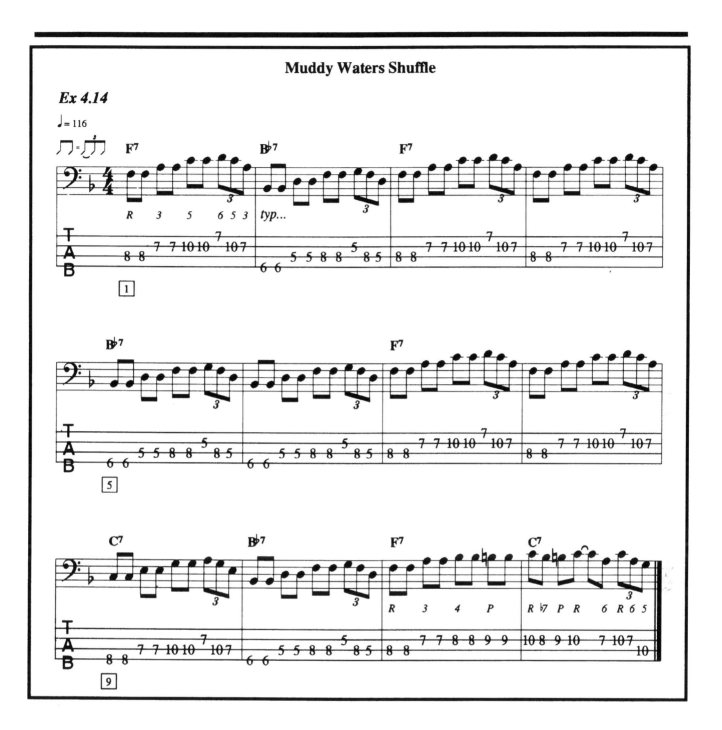

91

# Chicago Shuffle

## Rhythm and Blues ala Junior Wells

*Ex 4.16*

♩ = 108

## RHYTHM AND BLUES ................................................................

As you saw in Exercise 4.16, by mixing elements of the blues and funk, we have the beginnings of the style known as **Rhythm and Blues** (aka "R&B"). Early R&B was created by mixing arrangements from Chicago blues, Jump blues, and/or Mississippi Delta blues and then adding a dash of funk to the rhythm figures. While many blues artists have written and performed R&B versions of their songs, the more popular R&B artists were not considered "blues" artists. In fact, Rhythm and Blues is often thought of without paying homage to its debt to the blues. *"What did he say??"* I said that when you're playing R&B, don't forget that it is still the blues!! The rhythmic figures are the primary difference. Most of the classic R&B songs still follow one of the basic 12-bar blues progressions.

Exercises 4.17, 4.18, and 4.19 are examples of rhythm and blues bass lines you might find in records by Freddie King, Albert King, and Aretha Franklin. Again, note the use of the root, fifth, and flat seven chord tones in R&B bass lines.

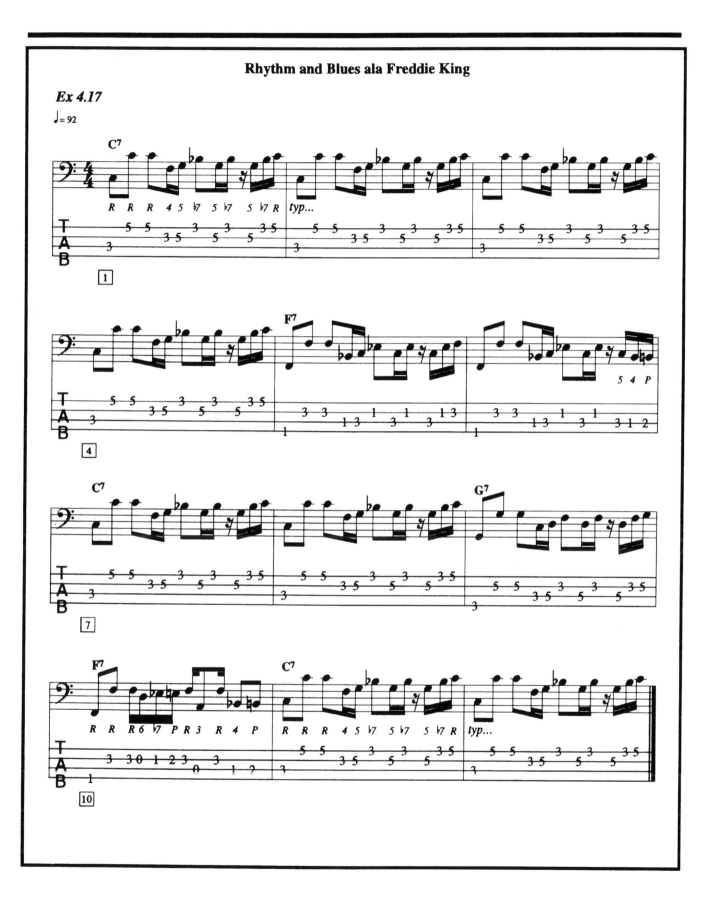

**Rhythm and Blues ala Aretha Franklin**

**Ex 4.18**

♩ = 84

# Rhythm and Blues ala Albert King

*Ex 4.19*

♩ = 88

**NOTE:** This bass line consists of a two-bar pattern defined in measures 1 & 2. This rhythmic pattern is adhered to for all chords, even in bars 9 and 10 where each chord is only played for one measure.

## SLOW BLUES STYLES ................................................................

I felt it was necessary to have a separate section to talk about playing slower blues bass lines. When the tempo drops, large gaps are created by the guitars, keyboards and vocals. As usual, the bass and drums must keep going. You will find that your choice of notes and rhythms is even more important. This is due to the fact that you are sticking out like a sore thumb, so you better be doing your job well!

We will take a look at four different approaches to playing slow blues. The first is Exercise 4.20 which is a simple example that emphasizes the root and fifth on the strong beats (one and three). The major 3rd is used to add some rhythmic "bounce" to the feel of the part. This would be the alternative to just playing half notes on the one and three with the root and third, respectively. The best piece of advice anyone could give you when developing slow blues bass lines is **keep it simple**. That space that the singer is leaving is helping to emphasize the vocal part and lyrics, not to give us musicians a chance to walk all over each other!

Exercise 4.21 is a pattern that is used frequently by Tommy Shannon (Stevie Ray Vaughan's bass player) in slow blues tunes. This pattern is similar to one of the Chicago patterns we saw earlier in that the ♭7 is emphasized on the third beat. This really drives that blues feel home, especially in a slower tune because the notes ring longer so that feeling really has a chance to sink in. Also, notice how it runs up to the fifth in the fourth beat. Once again the root, fifth, and flat seven are emphasized by this pattern.

99

Exercise 4.22 is an example of how ZZ Top approaches slow blues/rock most of the time. By shuffling on the root, a slow pulse is established and everything else lays nicely on top of the bass line. This is a great way to stay out of the way and just hold down the bottom. You may also notice that this progression has a slightly different turnaround in bars 9 and 10, making use of the minor 3rd chord (which is C7 in this case) in bar 9 and then doing a quick two-five turnaround in bar 10 (Bm7 to Em7). That's a nice change from the typical V7 to IV7 change we usually see there.

**Slow Blues ala ZZ Top**

*Ex 4.22*

Exercise 4.23 does a couple of new things. First of all, notice how it walks right down the mixolydian scale in each measure. This is a very cool bass line at any tempo. At slower tempos it can feel like you're falling of the edge of the world (and that would give anybody the blues, wouldn't it?). The other thing that happens is that the bass part and the guitar part come together on the fourth beat of bars 2, 6, 8, and 10 on a passing tone to emphasize the slide into the next chord. Approaching from a half-step above or below the target chord is a surefire way to imply the upcoming chord before you get there.

**Slow Blues ala Buddy Guy**

*Ex 4.23*

## ROCK BLUES ...........................................................................................................

As we have already seen, Rock 'n Roll draws heavily from the blues. This is done in a number of different ways. ZZ Top is a three-piece band from Texas that is undoubtedly a blues band that is playing and appealing to a primarily rock audience. Their songs are typically very blues-like in structure and feel, with the possible exception being that they tend to stay away from walking bass lines and stick with more of a straight shuffle groove as we will see in a minute.

Led Zeppelin is an English band that drew heavily from American blues artists like Willie Dixon, Howlin Wolf, and Muddy Waters. At second glance, though, you find that some of their most popular songs are far from a typical blues structure. Yet, they are still considered a blues-based rock band. Other bands like Bad Company have often been called blues/rock bands, yet many of their songs are not typical blues progressions.

The point here is that many different types of bands have taken elements and sounds of the blues and changed them enough to still sound bluesy, without actually being typically blues in structure or arrangement. We're talking about influences here. The Beatles have said that they were heavily influenced by American blues artists. Would you consider the Beatles to be a blues band? Neither would I, but they definitely have a blues influence in many of their songs.

In this section, we are going to focus on more traditional blues progressions using bass lines that may lend themselves better to a Rock 'n Roll setting than a blues setting. Exercise 4.24 is an example of how ZZ Top would approach a typical 12-bar blues progression. By shuffling on the root of the chord, the bottom is very solid and non-distracting. This exercise is written to be played as a triplet-shuffle feel, but try it as just straight eighth notes as well (no shuffle feel).

## Rock/Blues Shuffle

Exercise 4.25 is a similar example to be played as straight eighth-notes.  A common variation to driving the root note this way is to grab the 4th to the ♭3rd as shown on beat four of each measure.  The minor third (♭3) allows the bass part to emphasize the fact that this is a *blues* pattern because the minor third against a major chord will imply a bluesy sound or feel in the music.

Exercise 4.26 is another variation on the idea of using the 4th and ♭3rd at the end of each bar, except this time we are pedalling off of the root and ♭7 on the first three beats. This provides alot of movement, but at a slower tempo it really drives the groove home.

"Boogie" is a term that usually describes a feel similar to that of Jump Blues, but the bass line is usually played as straight eighth notes (no shuffle feel here). Early Jerry Lee Lewis records did this alot. The bass part would usually be doubled by the piano. Exercises 4.27 and 4.28 are examples of common 12-bar Boogie patterns.

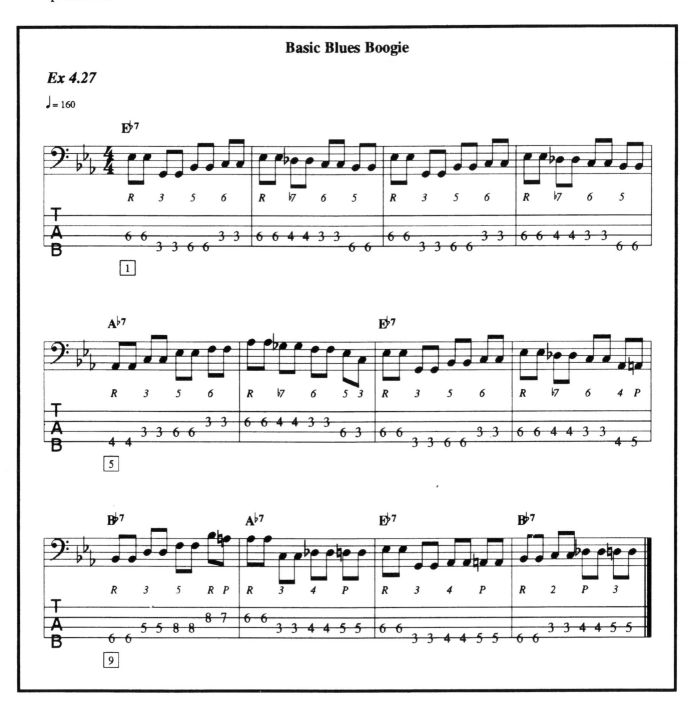

**More Blues Boogie**

*Ex 4.28*

Exercise 4.29 is basically a straight eighth note pattern with the exception of the third beat which uses a sixteenth/eighth figure to pickup the rhythm just a bit. Notice how the eighth note rhythm in bar 12 helps drive home the V7 chord before returning to bar 1.

**Straight Blues ala Albert King**

*Ex 4.29*

♩ = 112

Led Zeppelin helped pioneer the use of bluesy, minor pentatonic "riffs" in many of their blues based songs. One example of how they would approach this is shown in Exercise 4.30. This is a very mixolydian riff making use of the root, fifth, and flat seven chord tones before walking up from the major third to the fifth.

You will find many examples of the blues in Rock 'n Roll whether you are listening to pop/rock bands like Def Leppard and Bon Jovi, heavy metal bands Judas Priest and Deep Purple, and even alternative bands like Pearl Jam and Soundgarden. If you want to be a good rock bass player, it is to your advantage to have a firm grasp of how to play the blues.

## JAZZ BLUES

Many blues songs have been adapted to other styles of music including Rock, Country, Funk, R&B, and Jazz. When you apply jazz walking bass theory to blues chord progressions, you naturally get a very "jazzy" sounding blues song. But what does this really mean? First we must figure out what I mean by "jazz walking bass theory" (cuz we already know our standard blues progressions, don't we?)

Once again, I don't want to go into an in-depth theory discussion on a non-blues topic, but..... when creating walking bass lines in a jazz context, the best starting point is with the strong beat/weak beat concept I mentioned earlier. That is, the "strong" beats are 1 and 3, with the "weak" beats being 2 and 4. As before, we want to play our chord tones on the strong beats. However, when we pick our weak beat notes, we want to try and pick notes that lead into, or imply, the next chord *or chord tone* very clearly. This helps define the harmonic structure and definition of the song.

This means that we will be playing some notes that may not make sense against our current chord, but by looking ahead to the upcoming chord we will see that we are creating a more melodic walking bass part that has smooth transitions between chords. Typically, this is done by approaching the downbeat of the new chord from one half-step below, or one half-step above the chord tone we want to play on that downbeat.

The other aspect of playing jazz blues to consider is that there are some chord substitutions that take place to provide a more melodic change throughout the tune. We'll look at those in a few pages. First, let's look at some jazz walking bass lines over basic 12-bar blues changes. For the sake of simplicity, dominant seven type chords are about as complex as I want to get. If you want to pursue jazz walking bass lines, there are other books that are more appropriate.

OK, here we go. Exercises 4.31 and 4.32 are basic 12-bar blues progressions. Pay particular attention to the last note of each measure and its relationship to the first note of the next measure. Here's an example of how to do that in case you're confused (and this *is* confusing!): looking at bars 1 and 2 of Exercise 4.31, notice that the last note of bar one is a B♭. The first note of bar two is an E♭. B♭ is the fifth of E♭, so even though B♭ is the root of the current chord in bar one, it can also be viewed as the fifth of the next chord (which occurs at the beginning of bar two). In this case, the B♭ at the end of bar one is related to both the current chord and the next chord. That may not always be the case, but you won't know unless you figure it out.

## Jazz Walk (I-IV-V)

*Ex 4.31*

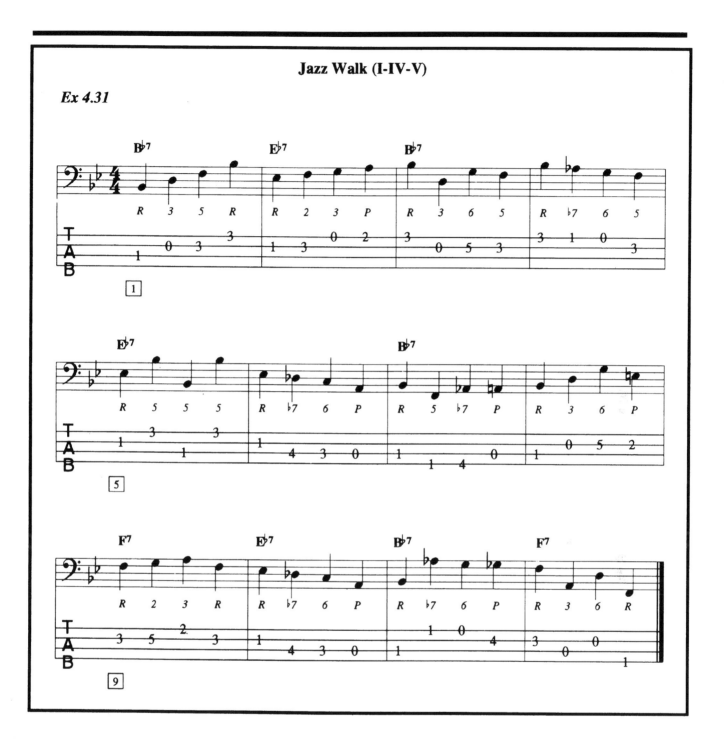

**Jazz Walk (I-IV-V)**

As with the Jump Blues style, it is not too uncommon to see a two-five turnaround in bars 9 and 10 of a basic 12-bar progression. We have already seen and played this a number of times. In Jazz Blues, there are some other alterations, or substitutions, that can be made as well. We are going to look at a couple of the common Jazz Blues progressions you will encounter. Table 4.1 explains what these new progressions will look like.

We can categorize them into two basic categories: the 6-2-5 progression and the 3-6-2-5 progression. This means that in bars 7, 8, 9, and 10 you will see the chord changes cycle from the six chord to the two chord to the five chord and resolving to the one chord in bar 11; thus the name "6-2-5" (or VI-II-V). Likewise, in bars 7, 8, 9, and 10 you may see the chords cycle from the three chord to the six chord, to the two chord, to the five chord and finally resolving to the one chord in bar 11; thus the name "3-6-2-5" (III-VI-II-V).

*Table 4.1*

# Jazz Blues Substitutions

## "6-2-5"

| Measure Number: | 1 | 2 | 3 | 4 |
|---|---|---|---|---|
| Chord: | I7 | IV7 | I7 | I7 |
| **Measure Number:** | 5 | 6 | 7 | 8 |
| Chord: | IV7 | IV7 | I7 | ivm7 |
| **Measure Number:** | 9 | 10 | 11 | 12 |
| Chord: | iim7 | V7 | I7 | V7 |

## "3-6-2-5"

| Measure Number: | 1 | 2 | 3 | 4 |
|---|---|---|---|---|
| Chord: | I7 | IV7 | I7 | I7 |
| **Measure Number:** | 5 | 6 | 7 | 8 |
| Chord: | IV7 | IV7 | I7 | iiim7♭5 / vim7 |
| **Measure Number:** | 9 | 10 | 11 | 12 |
| Chord: | iim7 | V7 | I7 | V7 |

Bars 11 and 12 can then either do the standard I-V turnaround that we've seen before or they may cycle through the 6-2-5 or 3-6-2-5 progression again. These are the next exercises we will look at. Exercise 4.33 shows you the 6-2-5 progression

**Jazz Walk (with VI-II-V)**

*Ex 4.33*

Theoretically, the six chord should be a minor seven chord as should the two chord. Sometimes, in an effort to reharmonize the melody, these chords may actually be played as dominant chords. If this is the case, you should try and approach each new chord (6, 2, 5, and 1) from one half-step below the root of the next chord as shown in Exercise 4.34. This helps to imply the upcoming chord and prepare the listener for the chord change.

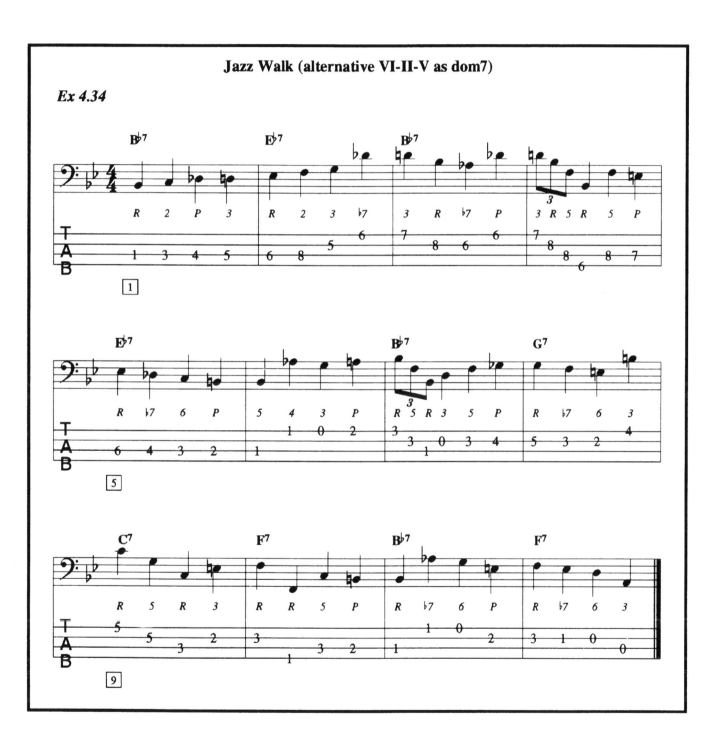

Exercise 4.35 shows you how the 6-2-5 is thrown in at bars 11 and 12 to complete the turnaround. Once again, in bars 11 and 12, notice the relationship between a note played on a weak beat (two or four) and the next note. This is the half-step below or above relationship I was speaking of earlier.

Jazz Walk (VI-II-V w/turnaround)

Ex 4.35

Exercises 4.36 and 4.37 are examples of common uses of the 3-6-2-5 progressions and turnarounds.

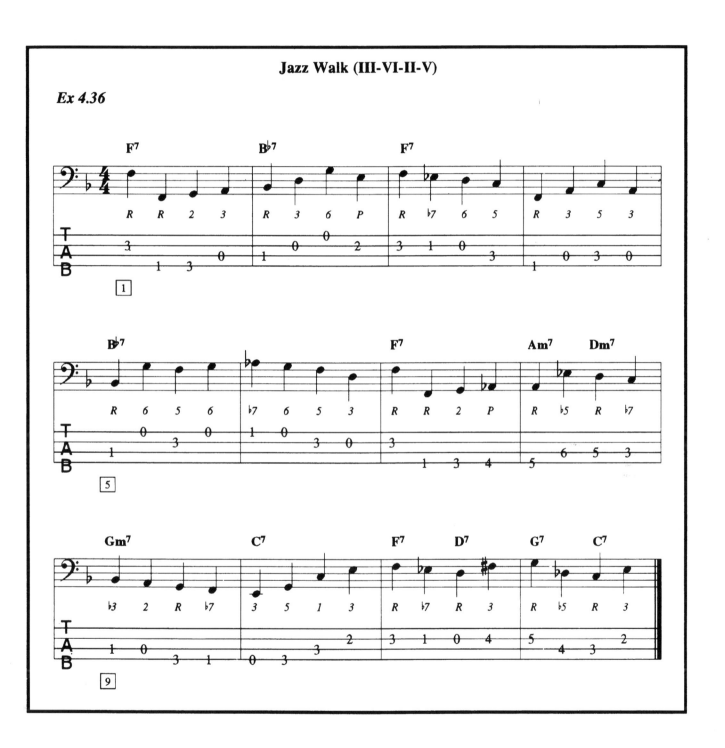

## Jazz Walk (III-VI-II-V  w/turnaround)

*Ex 4.37*

Exercise 4.38 contains some chord substitutions you may encounter as well. Notice the use of a diminished chord in bar six. You will also notice that bars 7 and 8 are slightly different as well. This is another series of substitutions that is very common (and one of my favorites, I might add...). Many arrangements of "Stormy Monday Blues" will use a variation on this progression.

# Intros, Endings, Turnarounds, and Fills

Unlike some other styles of music, you can expect to see specific phrases and chord progressions used as **intros** (the part of the song before the vocal starts), **endings** (typically the last 2 or 4 bars of the song), and **turnarounds** (the last 2 bars of the 8-, 12-, or 16-bar chord progression, just before the progression starts over again). There are also a number of common ways to get from the current chord to the next chord within the framework of the song. That is, how to get from the I7 chord to the IV7 chord and so on. I like to refer to these passages as **fills**.

In this chapter, we will take a look at a number of the typical intros, endings, turnarounds, and fills that you may encounter. It is a good idea to be very familiar with these different examples because you usually don't get alot of indication before the song starts as to what type of intro or ending you are going to be playing. Many times, someone just starts counting off the song and you're on your own! By listening and being aware of what others are playing, you can usually anticipate the intro and ending as you approach them - *provided*, of course, that you have studied this chapter and have a library of ideas to pull from!!

**INTROS** ....................................................................................................

Let's take a look at twelve different **intros** that are very common in the blues. You will notice that a few of them will be the same chord progression, but your choice of notes and rhythms will help make them sound different.

The first intro is Exercise 5.1 in which we play the major walking pattern over four bars. **Remember:** this intro phrase is *added* to the beginning of the song, meaning it <u>is not</u> part of the basic 12-bar blues chord progression (or whatever progression will follow). After the four bars in Ex. 5.1 you would start the 12-bar progression.

Exercise 5.2 is an example where the intro is 12-bars long, usually a guitar solo would be played over those twelve bars. The interesting thing here is that you just play the downbeat in each of the first four bars. This leaves space for the soloist to begin the song with the solo. Then, the whole band would kick in at bar 5 and play through the rest of the 12-bar progression. Jimi Hendrix' "Red House" began in similar fashion, with Jimi playing the first four bars by himself and the band comes in on the IV7 chord in bar 5 of the progression.

121

Another common intro progression is to play the I7 chord all the way until the last two beats before the verse starts. The V7 chord is played for those last two beats to give the song a "lift" just before the verse. As you will see, there are a couple of different approaches to this type of intro. Exercises 5.3 and 5.4 are examples of two of them.

Exercise 5.5 is similar to the last two examples, except this time the V7 chord is preceded by a "passing" chord that is one half-step above the V7 chord. The whole band would be playing this chord with you to emphasize the V7 chord when you get there. The passing chord can approach the V7 chord from either one half-step below ($\flat$V7) or above ($\sharp$V7) the V7 chord as shown in Exercise 5.6. (Also, the eighth note triplets in the first bar of Ex. 5.5 help set up a Texas shuffle feel for the rest of the song.)

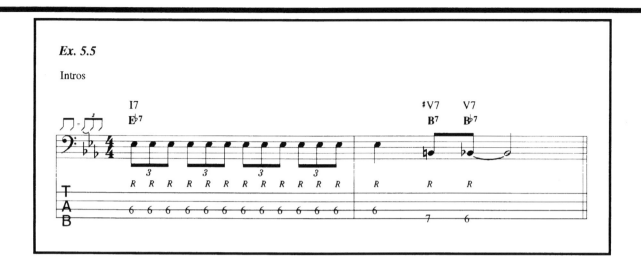

**Ex. 5.5**

Intros

**Ex. 5.6**

Intros

In Exercise 5.7 you see a slight variation on the last example. The V7 chord may be played on the downbeat of the last bar of the intro, then slide up one half-step to the passing chord, and then resolve back down to the V7 chord.

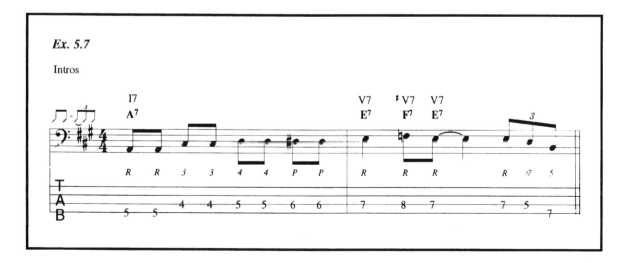

**Ex. 5.7**

Intros

Sometimes the intro may be four bars long. A common progression in this case is shown in Exercise 5.8. It makes use of the three commonly used chords in basic blues progressions, thereby setting up the listener's ear for the rest of the song.

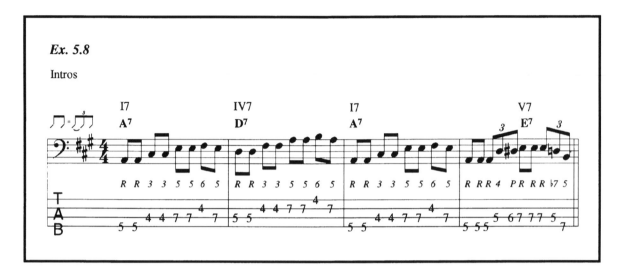

Exercise 5.9 is similar to Ex. 5.8, but it is only two bars long. This type of intro is more common in slower blues songs. If the tempo is too fast, the chords go by too fast to be properly heard and felt.

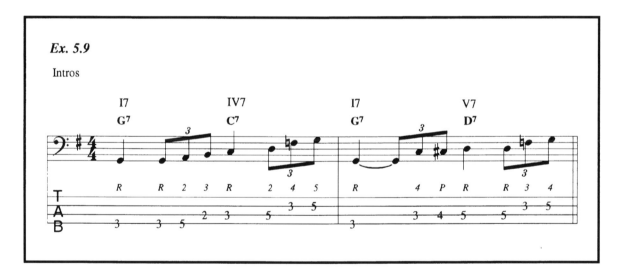

In Jazz Blues arrangements it is common to throw in the 6-2-5 turnaround we saw in the last chapter right at the beginning of the song. Exercise 5.10 is an example of this. At slower tempos the triplets will work just fine, but at faster tempos you may want to try and simplify the transition from one chord to the next. (Playing only one note from the triplets that I have written would be one way to do that.)

*Ex. 5.10*

Intros

Exercises 5.11 and 5.12 are examples of intros that are the same as bars 9 through 12 of your basic 12-bar progression. By doing this at the beginning of the song, every time you do it within the song the listener is prepared to go to the beginning of the verse because that's what they have heard before.

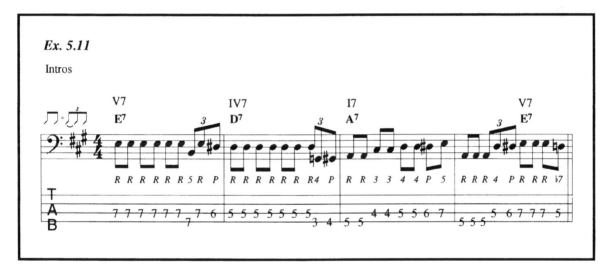

*Ex. 5.11*

Intros

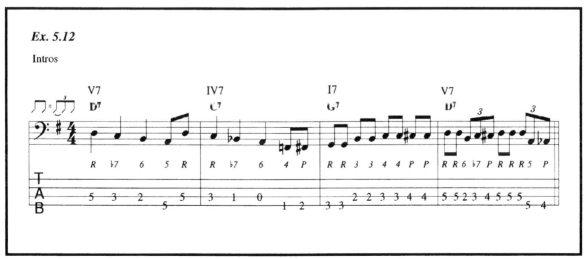

*Ex. 5.12*

Intros

Now we'll look at a number of different ways to get from one chord to the next. The first question to ask is, "how do I know what notes to use?" There are three steps to follow. First, identify scale and/or chord tones that lie between the current chord and the next chord. If you use only scale or chord tones, your **fills** will have a very happy, yet boring sound to them. This is because you are playing notes that the ear expects to hear. We have all heard scales before, so once you start playing up and down the scale the ear starts to assume that you are just playing scales. And you are. *Bo-ring!*

The second step is to look for passing tones that lie between the scale and chord tones you identified in step one. These passing tones will cause your fill to go outside of the scale for a moment or two. This will cause the listener's ear to take notice. The use of passing tones then opens you up to other scale and chord tone possibilities. The more you do this, the more you will start to hear that you can choose different notes.

The third step involves the rhythm figures you play. Sometimes by changing the rhythm figure a little you can pick the song up and carry it into the new chord. We will see examples of all three steps in this section, so pay close attention to the chord tones shown below the staff in each example as well as the rhythm figures and how they may change slightly from the established pattern.

The first change we will talk about occurs in bars 1-2 and bars 4-5 of a basic 12-bar progression. This is where the I7 chord goes to the IV7 chord. We will look at fills in this way and then in our final chapter you will see how it all gets put together. Exercises 5.13, 5.14, and 5.15 are examples of fills you could use to get from the I7 to the IV7 chord.

**NOTE:** As you go through these exercises, be aware that we are studying how to go *from* the I7 chord *to* the IV7 chord. In most of the exercises in this chapter the notes that occur in the second measure of each example are insignificant and are just there to complete the phrase. You should be concentrating on the notes in the first measure of each exercise unless I make specific mention otherwise.

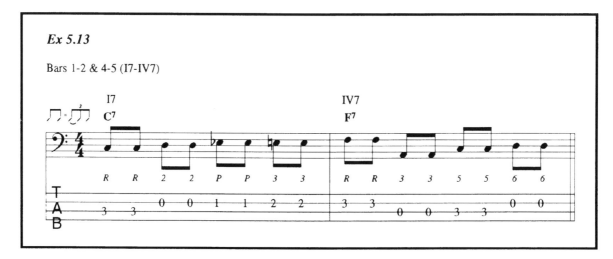

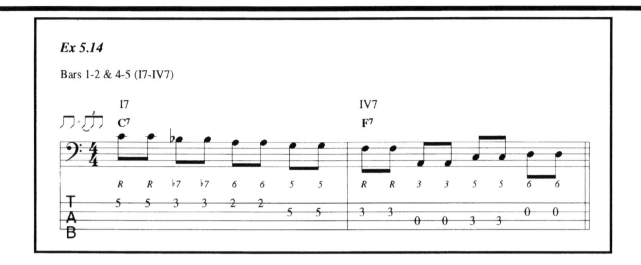

*Ex 5.14*

Bars 1-2 & 4-5 (I7-IV7)

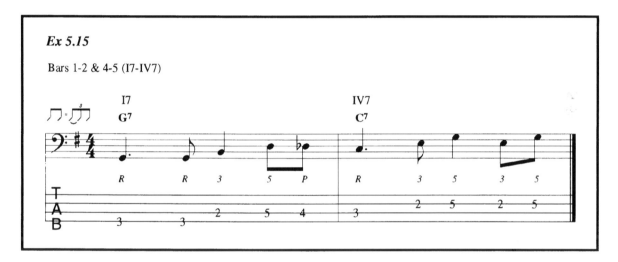

*Ex 5.15*

Bars 1-2 & 4-5 (I7-IV7)

As you can see in Exercises 5.16, 5.17, and 5.18 sometimes you need passing tones to get from one chord to the next and, as seen in Exercise 5.19, sometimes the chord tones work just fine by themselves. These four exercises relate to bars 2-3 and 6-7 in a basic 12-bar progression and go from the IV7 chord back to the I7 chord.

*Ex 5.16*

Bars 2-3 & 6-7 (IV7-I7)

*Ex 5.17*

Bars 2-3 & 6-7 (IV7-I7)

*Ex 5.18*

Bars 2-3 & 6-7 (IV7-I7)

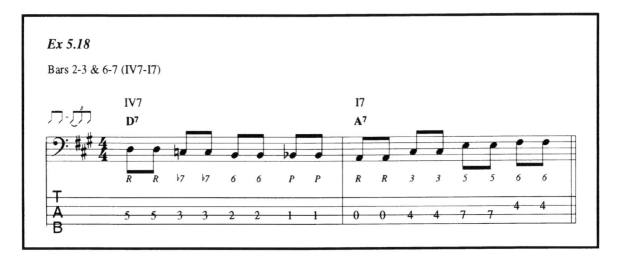

*Ex 5.19*

Bars 2-3 & 6-7 (IV7-I7)

128

Exercises 5.20, 5.21, and 5.22 go from the I7 chord in bar 8 to the V7 chord in bar 9 of your basic 12-bar progression. Again, sometimes you need two or three passing tones, and other times you may just need one to get you to the next chord.

*Ex 5.20*

Bars 8-9 (I7-V7)

*Ex 5.21*

Bars 8-9 (I7-V7)

*Ex 5.22*

Bars 8-9 (I7-V7)

Exercises 5.23, 5.24, and 5.25 deal with bars 9-10 when the progression is from the V7 chord to the IV7 chord. Being that these chords are only a whole step apart on your fretboard, you need to look to other parts of the scale to find notes to use and then add some passing tones to help it move properly.

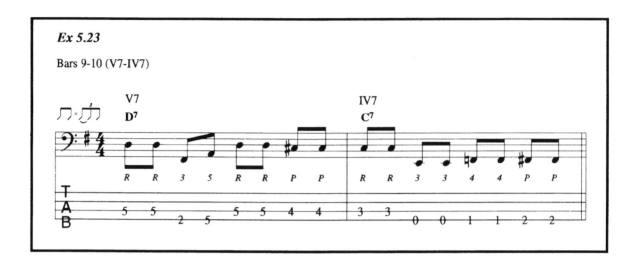

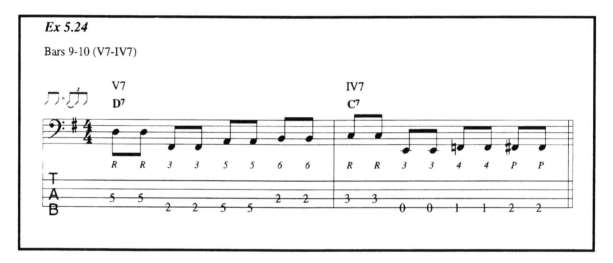

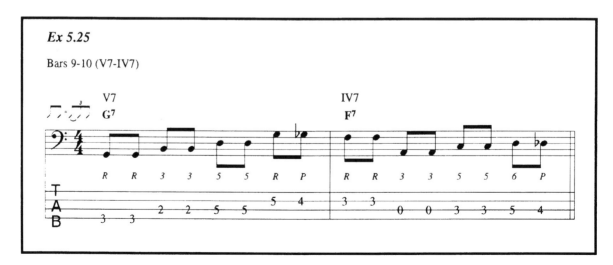

Bars 9-10 may also be the II7-V7 (2-5) turnaround as we saw earlier (especially in Jump Blues and Boogie tunes). Exercises 5.26 and 5.27 address this progression. In these examples we can take a look at the second measure in each exercise and think about those notes for a minute. When you have a 2-5 progression, they may be used together to create one melodic line that takes you back to the I7 chord (after the 2-5). In Ex. 5.26, the next chord after the 2-5 would be a C7. Notice how after walking up from the II7 chord to the V7, you then walk down through the V7 chord ending on the fifth, which is D. The next measure would be C7, and you are in perfect position to start that measure on the root, which is C.

Exercise 5.27 is similar except that you walk up through the V7 chord such that you end on the B natural and are ready to start the next measure on the C, which is again the root of the I7 chord. Get it? This usually how you will want to approach the 2-5 progression in bars 9-10.

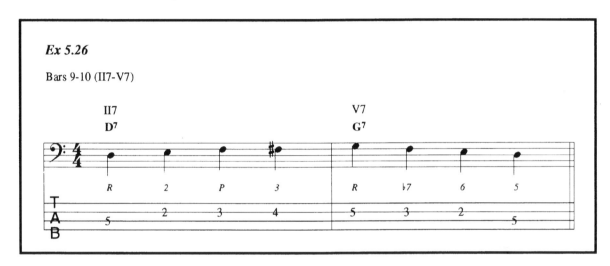

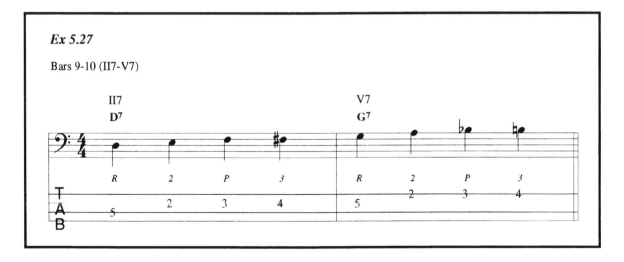

Bars 11-12 of the progression are commonly referred to as the **turnaround** because it is at this point that the song is about to go back to the beginning of the verse. (You are turning around from the end back to the beginning.) Exercises 5.28 through 5.32 show the most common I7 to V7 turnarounds. Exercise 5.33 uses the IV7 chord in bar 11 as well as the I7 and V7 in bars 11 and 12. In all of these exercises you definitely want to pay attention to what is happening in the second measure (which represents bar 12 of the progression) because this is leading you back to the I7 chord at bar 1 of the basic 12-bar progression. So, pay attention to how you're getting back to the beginning as well as how to get through bars 11 and 12.

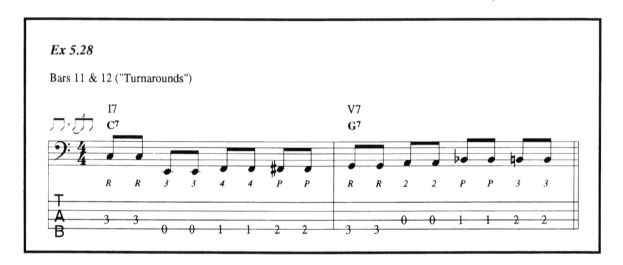

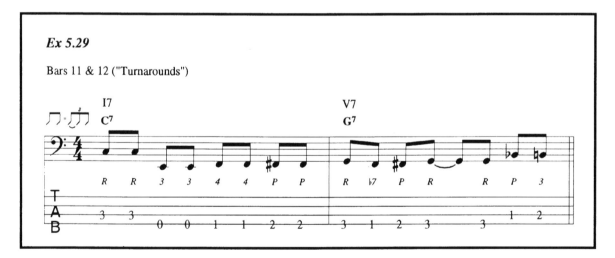

**Ex 5.30**

Bars 11 & 12 ("Turnarounds")

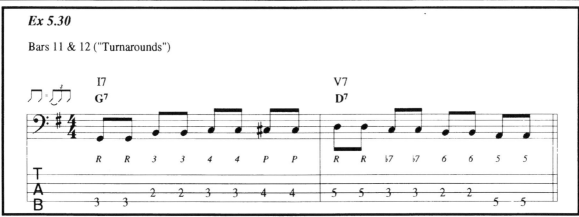

**Ex 5.31**

Bars 11 & 12 ("Turnarounds")

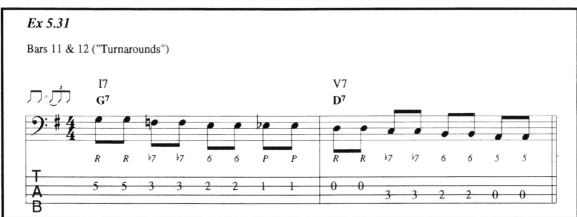

**Ex 5.32**

Bars 11 & 12 ("Turnarounds")

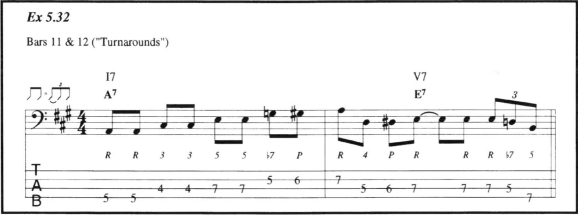

**Ex 5.33**

Bars 11 & 12 ("Turnarounds")

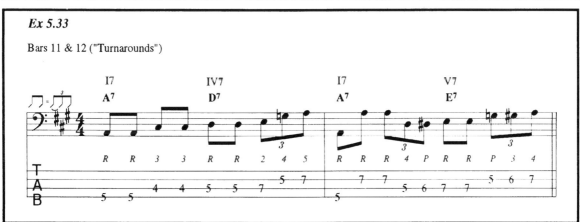

## ENDINGS ...................................................................................

Blues songs typically end during the final four bars of the progression, which is bars 9 through 12 in most cases. As we saw in the fills and turnaround sections, there are some different chord progressions that can occur in those different measures. The other factor is that we are ending the song, so there needs to be some drama. This helps to bring the song to its final climax.

Adding this sense of drama to the ending can be done by stopping on specific beats and letting the singer or guitar player wail through the bar(s) by themselves, or simply by increasing volume and intensity with which you play through the changes.

Exercises 5.34 through 5.45 demonstrate some of the more common endings in the blues. Note the use of the half-step approach chords in the last measure of many of the examples. This is the most common way to end the song. Also, notice where the last note is hit rhythmically. Many times it is "pushing" the third beat. Sometimes right on the beat, but it pushes in most cases.

134

## Ex 5.36

Endings: Bars 9-12

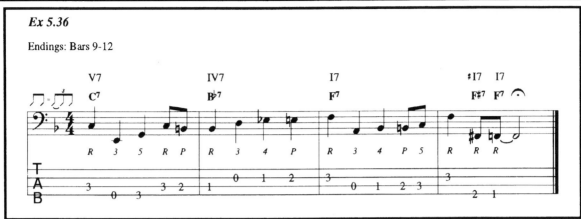

## Ex 5.37

Endings: Bars 9-12

## Ex 5.38

Endings: Bars 9-12

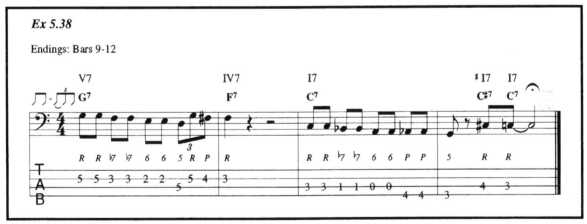

## Ex 5.39

Endings: Bars 9-12

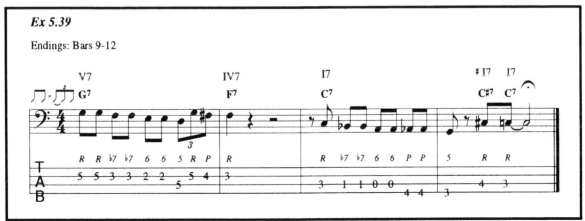

## Ex 5.40

Endings: Bars 9-12

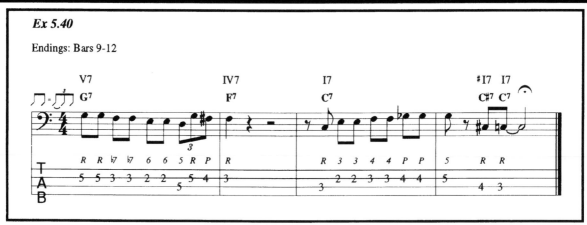

## Ex 5.41

Endings: Bars 9-12

## Ex 5.42

Endings: Bars 9-12

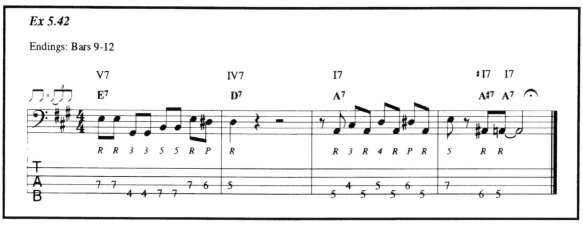

## Ex 5.43

Endings: Bars 9-12

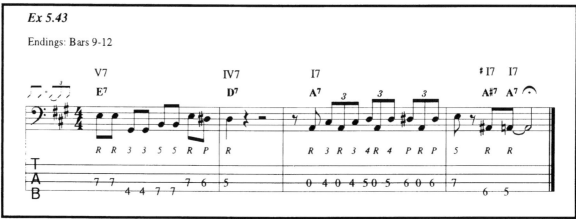

**Ex 5.44**

Endings: Bars 9-12

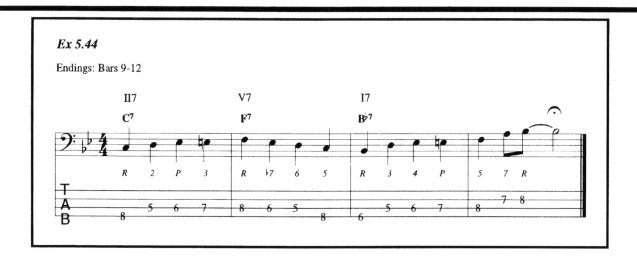

**Ex 5.45**

Endings: Bars 9-12

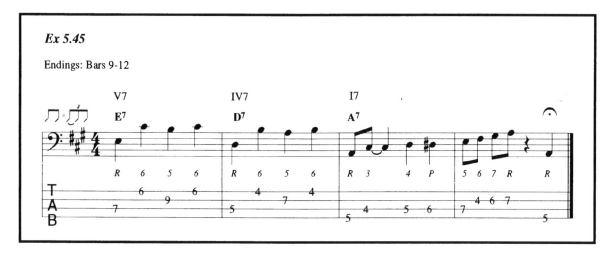

OK, so we've talked about the intros, the endings, and everything that happens in between. You know what that means? That's right, it's time to put it all together and play the blues. Let's go......

# Advanced Blues Bass Lines

BLUES REVIEW ..............................................................................................................................

This is where the fun really begins. The following 35 exercises all have an intro, two verses, and an ending. The idea here is to get used to playing all the way through a song and sticking to the groove.

As a bass player, establishing and maintaining the groove should be your main concern. You are providing the foundation upon which the entire song is going to be built. Therefore, it is your job to play strongly and consistently throughout the entire song. In order to do this, you need to play with confidence and this confidence comes from your knowledge and understanding of the blues and the chord progressions.

This does not mean that you don't get your chance to stray from the groove and take the song in another direction, or provide a different type of support during a solo or last verse. But, let's not start talking about running before we can walk. You must be able to get through the basic progressions over and over again, without wavering or getting out of whack. This is why most all blues bass lines are fairly simple and repetitive. You want to establish the groove and keep driving it home.

So, as you play through these exercises, remember how important it is to play them consistently and keep it simple. If you want to try and make some changes, go ahead. But make sure you can play them as written first! Also, you can try experimenting in other keys as well. Have fun with them, but don't forget how important it is to be able to play these types of patterns and songs without even thinking about it. When you can go through the progressions on "autopilot" that will free up your mind to concentrate on the more subtle aspects of playing such as the feel and overall emotion of the song. Ultimately, that's the goal. But you gotta have the tools and knowledge first!

OK, OK..... enough of me yacking already. Let's play.....

## 12-bar Southern Rock Blues

*Ex 6.1*

**8-bar Slow Blues Shuffle**

*Ex. 6.2*

Ex 6.3

## 12-bar Rock/Blues Shuffle

*Ex 6.4*

*Ex 6.5*

## Slow Blues in 6/8

*Ex 6.6*

*Ex 6.7*

*Ex 6.9*

**16-bar Jump Blues**

*Ex 6.10*

## 12-bar Shuffle

**Ex 6.12**

# 12-bar Rock Blues

*Ex 6.13*

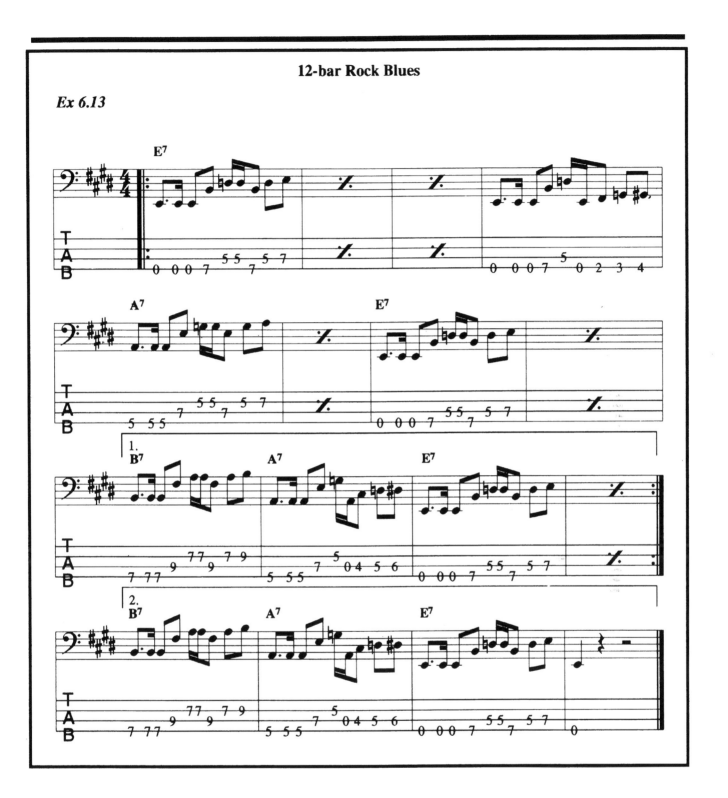

## 12-bar Jump Blues

*Ex 6.14*

## Slow Texas Shuffle

Ex 6.15

153

**Ex 6.16**

## 12-bar Slow ZZ Blues

*Ex 6.17*

Ex 6.18

# 12-bar Chicago Shuffle

Ex 6.19

## 12-bar Memphis Groove

Ex 6.20

*Ex 6.22*

## 12-bar Slow Shuffle

*Ex 6.23*

**12-bar Muddy Waters Shuffle**

*Ex 6.24*

# 12-bar Uptempo Swing

**Ex 6.25**

Buddy Guy Boogie

*Ex 6.26*

NOTE: "N.C." means "no chord" is played on this beat.  Usually, you and the entire band would be playing the same lick at that point.

## 8-bar Shuffle

# 12-bar Hoochie Koochie Blues

**Ex 6.28**

# 12-bar Boom Boom Blues

*Ex 6.29*

## 12-bar Blues/Rock Shuffle

*Ex 6.30*

## 12-bar Straight Rock/Blues

*Ex 6.31*

## 8-bar Rock/Blues

**Ex 6.32**

## 12-bar Rock Blues

*Ex 6.33*

*Ex 6.34*

## 16-bar West Coast Minor Blues

*Ex 6.35*

These next ten exercises take everything one step further.  Now, we add in the idea that you can make some changes to help take a song into different feels and levels of intensity.  This is usually done during a solo or breakdown of some kind as it would be too distracting during a verse.

To this end, I have constructed examples that have an intro, a verse, then what could be a solo section.  Then you repeat back to the verse again and then into the solo again (solely for the sake of repetition).  At the end of this second solo, you go into the ending.  Here goes ..... have fun!

**12-bar Rhythm & Blues**

*Ex 6.36*

175

## 12-bar Rock/Blues ala SRV

*Ex 6.37*

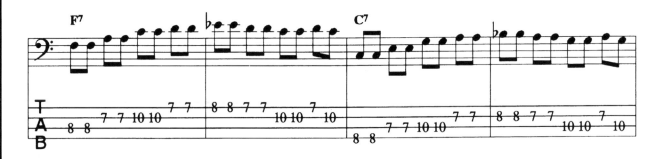

## 12-bar Texas Shuffle

*Ex 6.38*

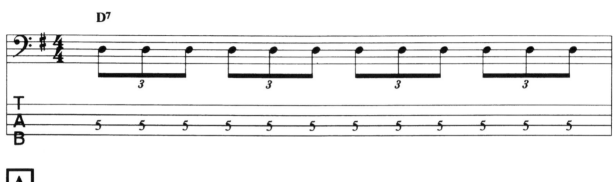

**A**

## 12-bar Jazz Blues

*Ex 6.39*

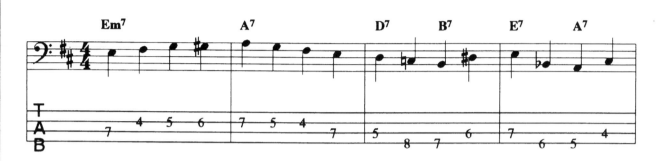

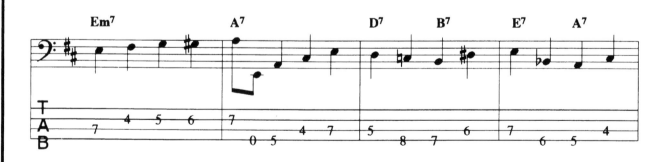

# Driving 12-bar Shuffle

*Ex 6.40*

**A**

## Slow Blues in 12/8

*Ex 6.41*

## 12-bar Texas Shuffle

*Ex 6.42*

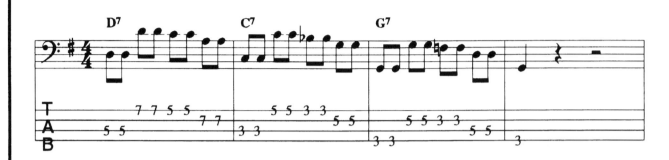

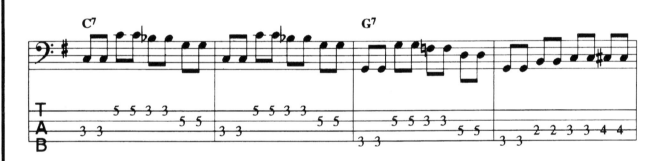

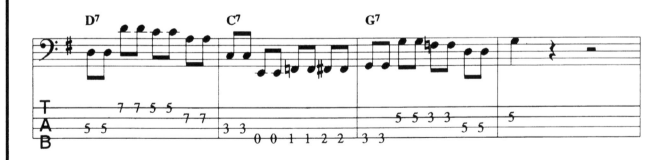

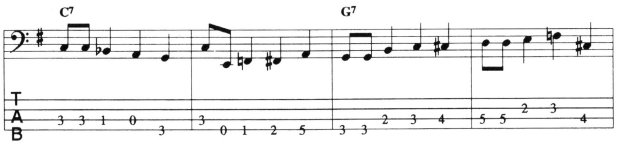

*Ex 6.43*

## 12-bar Slow Jazz Blues

*Ex 6.44*

This last example needs a little explantation.  It starts with a 12-bar progression which is a guitar solo (section 'A').  Then the verse (section 'B'), which repeats twice, is an 8-bar progression.  Then repeat back to the solo and then a couple of verses to end the song.  Buddy Guy did an arrangement like this for his song "Mary Had A Little Lamb".  You will occasionally find songs that mix 12-bar and 16-bar or 8-bar progressions.  They are fairly rare, but it does happen.

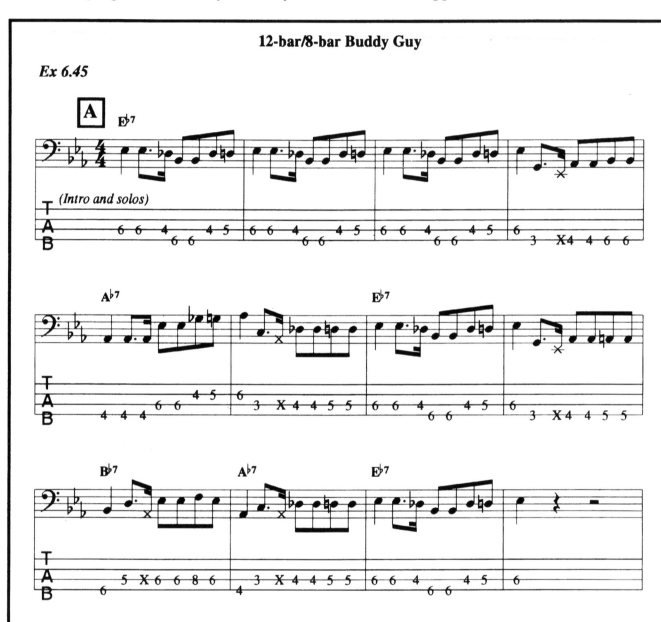

192

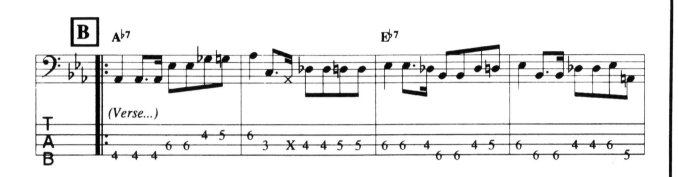

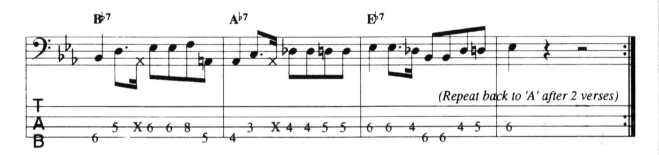

# Now What?

Well, at this point (if we both have done our jobs correctly) you should have a very solid understanding of how to play blues bass. You have the information to draw from, the only thing you can't get out of a book is experience. That, you have to get for yourself.

How do you do that? Well, first of all the best experience is playing in a band situation. Here are a couple of recommendations for you to consider. At a minimum, it usually isn't too hard to round up a couple of musicians to get together and play the blues. (I don't know too many guitar players who pass up the opportunity to solo all day while the rest of the band just grooves!) Get a guitar player and a drummer and even a keyboard or piano player if one is available. The blues is definitely one style of music where you can even add horn players if you know some. They would probably jump at the chance to play. The cool thing about getting together to jam some blues is that you don't really need a singer. (This is cool because good singers are usually very hard to find!) You can just have the guitars, keyboards, and horns trade solos. This gives you, the bass player, a great opportunity to practice some different walking approaches and try some different feels and patterns without causing too much distraction. What a great way to experiment!

It is also fairly common to find blues jams at local bars and clubs. Many times they are on Sunday afternoons or evenings. If you can't find any, talk to some of the club owners about starting one. They're always looking for an excuse to get people into the club!

Start a blues band. It's really not that hard to do. The songs are already written, you just have to learn them. Blues bands are extremely fun to play in, people usually enjoy going to see them, and you can make some extra money most of the time. Sounds like a number of good reasons right there!

The other thing to do, and this is very beneficial, is to get as many blues recordings as you can and learn the bass lines to **all** of the songs. Learning as many different songs as possible will only help to increase your understanding of blues bass lines, make you even more familiar with standard blues bass lines, and give you new ideas to build from. To that end, "Appendix A" on the next page has a list of some of my favorite blues records.

Basically, the message is: *play the blues as much as possible.* Now, I'm no doctor, but I believe this philosophy will lead to a longer, happier life for all of us. At least, that's what I want to believe.

Thanks for buyin' the book, and good luck!  ...... Mike H.

# Appendix A

This is a list of some of my favorite blues records, and naturally many of them were used in my research for this book. As Joliet Jake says on the Blues Brothers <u>Briefcase Full Of Blues</u> record, *"I suggest you buy as many blues albums as you can."* Sounded like good advice to me, so I'll pass it along to you! Due to the fact that blues records have been around for years and have never been chart busters quite like rock and pop records, it can be hard to find specific records. But, the good news is that the blues is getting more and more popular in recent years, which means that more and more stores are carrying a larger selection of blues records, tapes, and CDs.

| Artist | Title | Label | Cat. Number |
|--------|-------|-------|-------------|
| Allman Brothers Band | *Eat A Peach* | Polydor | 823654 |
| | *Live At Fillmore East* | Polydor | 823273 |
| | *Seven Turns* | Epic | 46144 |
| Atlantic R&B 1947-1974 | CD Box Set | Atlantic | 82305 |
| The Blues Brothers | *Briefcase Full of Blues* | Atlantic | 19217 |
| Blues Masters | *Vol 2 - Postwar Chicago* | Rhino | 71122 |
| | *Vol 3 - Texas Blues* | Rhino | 71123 |
| | *Vol 5 - Jump Blues Classics* | Rhino | 71125 |
| | *Vol 8 - Mississippi Delta Blues* | Rhino | 71130 |
| Eric Clapton | *From The Cradle* | Reprise | 45735 |
| Willie Dixon | *I Am The Blues* | Columbia | MFCD872 |
| Robben Ford | *Talk To Your Daughter* | Warner Bros | 25647 |
| Guitar Player Magazine | *Legends of Guitar -* | | |
| | *Electric Blues Volume 1* | Rhino | 70716 |
| Buddy Guy | *Damn Right I've Got The Blues* | Silvertone | 41462 |
| | *Feels Like Rain* | Silvertone | 41498 |
| | *Live in Montreaux* | | |
| | *(with Junior Wells)* | Evidence | 26002 |
| Jimi Hendrix | *Live At Winterland* | Rykodisc | RCD20038 |
| Albert King | *The Best Of Albert King* | Stax | FCD-60-005 |
| B.B. King | *Live At The Apollo* | GRP | 9637 |
| Freddie King | *(1934-1976)* | Polydor | 831817 |
| Led Zeppelin | *Led Zeppelin* | Atlantic | 19126 |
| | *Led Zeppelin II* | Atlantic | 19127 |
| | *Led Zeppelin III* | Atlantic | 19128 |
| Little Walter | *The Best Of Little Walter* | MCA | CHD9292 |
| Stevie Ray Vaughan | *Soul To Soul* | Epic | 40036 |
| | *Couldn't Stand The Weather* | Epic | 39304 |
| | *Live Alive* | Epic | 40511 |
| | *In Step* | Epic | 45024 |
| | *The Sky Is Cryin'* | Epic | 47390 |
| Muddy Waters | *Live At Mr. Kelly's* | MCA | CHD9338 |
| Johnny Winter | *Second Winter* | Columbia | 9947 |
| | *Let Me In* | Pointblank/ | |
| | | Charisma | 91744 |
| ZZ Top | *Deguello* | Warner Bros | 3361 |

*Great Music at Your Fingertips*